# In-Hand

# In-Hand

## A Practical Guide
## to Preparing & Showing
## Your Horse

K.J. FitzGerald

Half Halt Press, Inc.
Boonsboro, Maryland

# In-Hand
## A Practical Guide to
## Preparing & Showing Your Horse

*Copyright© 2002 K.J. FitzGerald*

Published in the United States of America by
HALF HALT PRESS, INC.
P.O. BOX 67
BOONSBORO, MD 21713
www.halfhaltpress.com

Book, book jacket design and production by
DESIGN POINT STUDIO, Epping, NH

Front Jacket Photo by Sonya S. Barry. Rosette courtesy of Hodges Badge Company, Inc. For more information on products or a copy of a catalog, contact Hodges Badge Company, Inc., P.O. Box 1290, Portsmouth, RI 02871. T: 800-556-2440, F: 800-292-7377, E: info@hodgesbadge.com or visit on-line at www.hodgesbadge.com

Library of Congress Cataloging-in-Publication Data

Fitzgerald, K. J., 1962-
    In-hand : a practical guide to preparing & showing your horse / K.J. Fitzgerald.
       p. cm.
    ISBN 0-939481-63-4
    1. Horses--Showing. 2. Horse shows. I. Title.

SF294.5 .F58 2002
636.1'0811--dc21
                                                         2002038798

This book is dedicated to

My first and only husband STEVE who from our inno-
cent, naive beginnings believed me when I said I
wanted to be a writer. He alone encouraged me and gave me
the chance.

To DAN STREETER who is one of those people I care
deeply about though we have never met. He is the editor every
budding writer dreams of, the one who offers a double-edged
sword— the bloodthirsty red pen and the courage to fly.

Thanks to the following people:

To Mike Rowe for patiently sharing his vast knowledge of
hunters.

To Bob Orton, who was the first to open my eyes to the world
of sporthorses.

To Deri Jeffers and Allison Turner for my dressage inspira-
tions.

To Hilda Gurney for sharing her thoughts and opinions.

To the many judges, horse owners, breed associations, USDF
and sporthorse handlers for sharing their opinions, information and adventures.

# Contents

# Chapter One
## Showing Horses in-Hand

The horse is loved for his grace and beauty. Part of the lure for horse lovers is being able to become part of that graceful animal through riding him. The basics of riding begin before the saddle ever crosses the horse's back.

A well-mannered horse is a prize and is fairly easy to create through training. The benefits of learning the training techniques for preparing a horse to show in-hand extend far beyond the show ring. Not only is it a thrill to be able to run at full speed beside a horse that stays at one's shoulder on a loose rein, but it builds trust and respect between the handler and the horse. A horse that consistently stays at his handler's shoulder, in any gait and through turns, is a breeze to work with, from bringing him in from the pasture to grooming. As the horse learns to move forward when asked, ease of communication will translate smoothly, making the transition to under saddle training and trailer loading almost effortless. Showing and handling such a horse is a pleasure. A horse with this type of training is well prepared, whatever his final career may be.

In-hand classes are held for horses as young as weanlings. Training and showing in these classes offers much to a young horse and his owner. There is every opportunity for the owner to learn the concepts of aids, including the seemingly mysterious concept of half halts, while the horse is still in-hand.

Familiarity with various showgrounds prepares a young horse for good behavior at these same grounds once under saddle. Top sporthorse handler Bob Orton of Gladys, Virginia, says horses exposed to showing at an early age are "show wise and light years ahead of other horses in their level of maturity."

Teaching the horse to perform in-hand allows the handler to move in unison with her horse, as the horse learns to stay at the handler's shoulder and to go willingly at the handler's chosen pace and direction. Still, many riders flounder when they are out of the saddle and on the ground. Instead of grace and elegance, the horse pulls the handler, the handler pulls the horse, the horse pushes the handler and so on. Shortcomings in this area are often never corrected and horses make their rounds from owner to owner without ever getting a firm grasp on ground manners.

# The Purpose of Showing In-Hand

The outcome of the judging in a breeding class, whether for sporthorses or hunters may or may not be prophetic. The judges make the best determination they can about the future by using the walk, trot and build of the horse that is presented at that time.

There are many factors that go into making a horse successful in his chosen career. Human talent, the training and the horse's mind make up at least three-quarters of the development of an upper-level dressage horse, jumper, driving horse, hunter or eventer. With sporthorses, the elements judged on the triangle end up being a small percentage of what will actually determine the horse's future. Still, they must not be dismissed as unimportant. Three good gaits are essential to any horse, as is the conformation that makes these gaits possible.

It's important to remember that the conformation of a young horse can go through drastic changes as he grows. Of the two gaits to be judged on the triangle or in hunter in-hand classes, the trot can be improved with training, and a walk can decline as training progresses. A decline in the walk is most apt to happen as a result of faulty training, but conformation type can predispose a horse to problems in his walk. Of the three elements that are judged, conformation, walk and trot all are subject to change.

Even a horse that has all the physical talent desired when fully mature depends on skilled training and an excellent rider before he can reach his full potential. A horse with physical shortcomings can overcome them if these latter two elements compensate. One other factor that determines a horse's future is his disposition. A horse's trainability, his desire to please his rider and his heart combine as the main deciding factors in his future. This is something that isn't fully known until the horse blossoms under saddle.

With the future blank, like a puzzle with missing pieces, when gaits and conformation are all that can be judged in a young horse at that time and they are the only measurement we can use to predict the future potential of the young horse, what is the purpose of in-hand classes? The reasons are many:

Breeders like to have the get of their stallions shown so that the public is aware of what their breeding program has to

*Happiness is having your breeding program recognized as successful when your baby wins in-hand.*

offer, rather than having to wait many years to see the results under saddle. In many cases it is not financially possible to wait years to profit from the sale of a stallion's offspring.

Some people show their horses in-hand to promote young prospects they have for sale. Others show to get a feel for how their breeding program compares to that of their competitors. Not all of these breeders expect a first-place ribbon to prove the worth of their efforts. Some breed for international prospects, others aim for the larger market of the lower levels.

Still others show their young horses in-hand to provide them with the experience of showing so that once under saddle they can proceed with the work at hand in the show

*Breeders like to have the get of their stallions to make the public aware of what their breeding program has to offer.*

ring, rather than spooking at all the new and strange surroundings. Other people show their young horses in-hand to promote a rare breed they have committed themselves to.

In this book, we'll look at the two main types of showing horses in-hand: "on the triangle" (sporthorses) and "on the line" (hunters).


## What is a Sporthorse?

Since there is often confusion about what a 'sporthorse' is, some clarification before we move on may be helpful. Any athletic equine could be considered a sporthorse, but the term is used most often when referring to horses used for dressage, eventing, driving or jumping. We'll refer most often to dressage in this book as most sporthorse competitions are held at dressage competitions and are judged by those standards.

Young prospects at these events are shown in-hand on the triangle, which is the pattern used to display the horse's movement and conformation. The judging is to determine their potential for dressage, though they may be destined for other disciplines.

Warmblood/Thoroughbred crosses are currently catching the judge's eye. They are not as heavy or coarse as the warmbloods with more distant Thoroughbred ties. The term warmblood technically refers to any horse that is not a coldblood (draft), or a hotblood (Akhal Teke, Thoroughbred or Arabian). More specifically, warmblood refers to European breeds, many of which descend from warhorses and coach horses and are strongly infused with Thoroughbred and Arabian blood.

It's important to note that the term sporthorse does not refer to a particular breed: any breed could, technically, be a sporthorse. It has more to do with the horse's "job," though certain types or breeds may be more disposed to being considered sporthorses.

The United States Dressage Federation (USDF) sponsors the All-Breeds Awards in which all the members of a certain breed registry compete against each other, despite their geographic location. Horses of the same breed in California can compete with horses in Pennsylvania by way of scores obtained at the level at which they are competing. This makes competing successfully on any breed possible.

While every breed and color of horse can be used in dressage or hunter classes, some are at a disadvantage. Color is an obstacle some horses have to overcome to make it in the show ring. Horses with uneven socks are considered distracting to watch, as is a horse with a crooked blaze. Buckskins, Palominos and other unusual colors are at a lesser disadvantage than the Pintos and Appaloosas, but with any of these horses, whether in the hunter or dressage ring, they are under more pressure than a run-of-the-mill bay to perform well and be at their best at all times. Unlike the bay, these horses will be remembered.

Many types of Paint markings give the illusion, good or bad, of certain conformation aspects. Areas most frequently affected by markings are the head, neck, shoulder and croup/hip. These areas can because of the markings look straight or thick when they are not. Some judges don't like to take the extra time to look past a Pinto's flamboyant markings to judge the conformation beneath.

We'll take a look at the in-hand showing of sporthorses, beginning with the next chapter. ❧

# Chapter Two
## Conformation

While a horse with few conformation faults may be more likely to stay sound, ideal conformation is not a blueprint for success. The best performing horse doesn't always have the best conformation.

The human definition of ideal conformation is something that changes with time. This can be seen in sporthorses where lighter, more agile horses are in vogue, whereas the heavier warmbloods were the rage during the latter part of the last century. In the Western breeds, changes in styles of conformation can be seen frequently, within just a few generations.

Nature's idea of ideal conformation is constant. Mustangs, Zebras, Przewalski's Horses and Fjords all have more similarities in conformation than not. The conformation of human design, through breeding programs, readily makes it to Grand Prix, but vastly different nature's horses have made it there as well, such as the Mustang JB Andrew and the Fjord Wez. Each animal should be looked at as an individual. There are many examples of horses that have made it to Grand Prix despite not being the right breed, the right size, or having the right conformation. Many of these brilliant horses would not have been well received by sporthorse judges had they been judged to meet a certain standard. Sporthorse judges today are advised to look at the whole horse as a unit, rather than at his components. Even so, it is doubtful that many of the world's best Olympic and Grand Prix horses would have pinned first in-hand in their younger days. Beauty is as beauty does. That is the secret to judging your own horse's conformation. Ultimately, the only faults in a sporthorse are those that interfere with the horse's performance.

## Insights on Judging

A method of determining whether a horse's conformation is balanced is to divide the horse into three sections. Each section should be equal in length to the next. The first section is from the head to the shoulder, the second from the shoulder to the hip and the last is from the hip to the tail. The modern dressage horse should be rectangular from head to tail. The length, however, should not come from a long back, but from impressive shoulders and hindquarters. Lipizzans and other horses of classical build tend to be square rather than rectangular. Even this aspect of conformation is speculative.

## Head and Neck

For a horse intended for upper levels of dressage his mouth needs to be large enough to comfortably contend with two bits. The inside of the horse's mouth is what needs to be roomy, because even small breeds with delicate heads, such as Arabians and Morgans, can be shown with a double bridle.

The neck should rise up from the withers and tie in high to the chest. A slight ewe-neck, also known as an upside down neck, where the muscles bulge out from underneath, and the crest is weak and undeveloped, or a straight neck can often be improved with correct training, as the bugling muscles at the bottom of the horse's neck are commonly caused by improper riding. The throatlatch should be clean. This means shapely, curved and not too thick. A dressage horse would have trouble breathing while on the bit if the throatlatch is, excessively thick. Sometimes, if the horse's jowl is not thick, even though the throatlatch is, the horse will be able to manage being on the bit. A thick jowl combined with a thick throatlatch is very likely to cause problems however.

## Hindquarters

Many upper level riders and FEI judges feel that the most important positive aspect a dressage horse needs in his conformation is a well-muscled loin. A well-muscled loin helps a horse move through the back and develop *schwung*, or impulsion. This area located between his hips and back, should show the spine as an indentation due to muscles, not fat on either side. A thin horse is bound to show his spine, but if the horse is not thin and his spine rises up along his back, he will not have power in his movement.

It is always best to purchase a horse that is sound to begin with, unless you are assured that an existing problem is minor and temporary. A sound, well-muscled back, hindquarters and hocks are especially important to the dressage horse as they are under much stress and are the places most likely to develop problems. A strong back, hindquarters and hocks can also help offset other areas of weakness, such as too long a back or a weak neck.

From the horse's hip, to the point of his rear, to the stifle and back to the hip should make a nice, even triangle of ample size. This measurement speaks of the length of hip and strength of croup. A goose-rumped horse, or one with a short hip will have an irregular triangle. A wide, even triangle speaks of a good strong hip.

## Legs

Front and rear legs should be close to equal in length and short enough to give the horse a rectangular appearance. Long legs, while elegant, don't keep the horse well balanced in tight turns. The gaskin should not be straight and should be well muscled. The forearm should be long and muscled, the cannon bones short, and the knees straight, and flat. A long, forward sloping femur is desired as it gives the horse the ability to reach under himself.

Leg bones should be straight when viewed from the front or behind and not rotated or twisted, but this shouldn't be a strict requirement. Toed-in, in at the knees, bench-kneed, calf-kneed, entire leg turned out to the side, or cow-hocks, and sickle-hocks (which are often found together) are all faults that can all come on a horse that has good movement and remains sound.

## Hooves and Pasterns

Hooves are the foundation of every horse. Ideally, a hoof should be large enough to carry the size and weight of the horse it must bear. Most warmbloods have a large enough hoof. Some Thoroughbreds and Western breeds, such as the Quarter Horse, have individuals with hooves too small in comparison to the body.

Other problems with hooves that can affect the soundness of the hoof itself or cause strain on tendons and ligaments are contracted heels, flat feet, clubfoot, cracked walls and underslung heels.

Many undesirable aspects of the hoof can be corrected or at least reduced by a competent blacksmith. Although many of these faults are rumored to lead to possible lameness, many blacksmiths and veterinarians say that lameness does not necessarily visit an imperfect hoof more often than a more perfect one. A horse's soundness is dependent on many factors other than conformation, such as nutrition, environment, care and luck.

## Working Together

The angle from the hoof to the pastern should be a continuous line. The pastern should be of medium length. Too short often means a rough gait, and too long can be weak. A 45-degree angle is desired for both pastern and shoulder, and the angle of the these usually match. If the shoulder angle is difficult to determine, a glance at the pasterns can often be a guide for determining shoulder angle. Shoulder angle is measured from the top of the withers, along the scapula to the point of the shoulder and along the humorus.

A long back, long neck, short croup, short hip and/or a hind end that is higher than the withers are all considered areas of possible weaknesses in the dressage horse, since all of these areas determine the strength of impulsion and collection. Quarter Horse-type breeds are often built "downhill" (with the croup higher than the withers). Also common in these breeds are tremendous hindquarters with more than enough power to elevate the horse's front end. This is an example of a horse being able to compensate for his shortcomings. Another example of conformation that is undesirable in a dressage horse is a straight shoulder, because it can mean that a horse has limited reach. If the straight shoulder is combined with long forearms and a free elbow and if the shoulder does not restrict the horse's movement, then the shoulder should not be considered a fault. A long neck, long back, and upright gaskin, all can be compensated for by a long hip and muscular loin and hindquarters.

It is said that a small head is better for balance and for helping to keep weight off the forehand, but performances by horses such as the Olympic champion, Gifted, blow holes all through that theory. It is never fair to judge a horse by the way he stands or by his individual parts. The horse is an entire entity. How he presents himself as a complete package, how all the parts come together as a whole are what need consideration. The following is a chart of conformation faults and possible side effects that can result from them. This is not a complete list of all possible faults in a horse, but it does give an idea of the difference between good conformation and bad. This is only a guide and meant to give insight into what is ideal.

| IMPERFECTION | DESCRIPTION | POSSIBLE SIDE EFFECTS AND SOLUTIONS |
|---|---|---|
| **Hooves** | | |
| Clubfoot | One front hoof is dished and the heel is usually high. Blood vessels within the hoof are constricted and there is chronic inflammation and possible rotation of the coffin bone as in laminitis. This is thought to be a hereditary defect. | The horse may be lame due to the clubfoot. Lameness is permanent. A few clubfooted horses remain sound throughout their lives. If purchasing a horse with a clubfoot, an X-ray of the coffin bone is advisable. |
| Cracks in hoof wall | Cracks may be on the surface or deep and extend to the coronet band. Hoof color is not a determining factor in cracked hooves. Causes are | Though cracks can cause lameness if unattended, they can be successfully dealt with. Make sure the horse |

| IMPERFECTION | DESCRIPTION | POSSIBLE SIDE EFFECTS AND SOLUTIONS |
|---|---|---|
| Cracks (*cont.*) | numerous -from nutrition to environment. | gets a balanced diet. Hoof dressings can help protect hooves from swampy land. Shoes may help reduce cracking. |
| Underslung heels | The horse's toe is long and the heel almost nonexistent. This condition is probably hereditary. | The tendons are under considerable strain and can lead to bowed tendon. Shoes that raise the heels can fix the problem. |
| Contracted heels | The frog is narrow and the bulbs of the heels are small and close together. Hooves that are too small often have contracted heels. This can be hereditary, or caused by improper hoof care. | The hoof can become soreeasily. A blacksmith can spread the heels with springs or use a ¾ shoe to help spread the heels. |
| Hoof too small | The bulk of the horse is massivein comparison to the dainty hoof. Possibly inherited. | A tiny hoof is under more stress than one horse's size. Navicular is a highly feared possible result. |
| Legs | | |
| Pasterns short and upright. | The line between hoof and pastern is often broken, | Horse is prone to bowed tendons and ringbone. |

| IMPERFECTION | DESCRIPTION | POSSIBLE SIDE EFFECTS AND SOLUTIONS |
|---|---|---|
| Pasterns (cont.) | rather than the desired continuous line. Probably inherited. | Gaits are likely to be short and choppy making for an uncomfortable ride. |
| Pasterns too long | As in the short upright pastern, the line between the hoof and pastern is a broken, rather than a continuous line. Probably inherited. | Too long a pastern can break down with heavy use such as racing. Dropped pastern can result. |
| Toed-in | Hooves only may turn slightly in, or entire leg might turn in. Sometimes only be noticed during movement. Probably inherited. | Any variation in leg straightness can affect the visual appeal of movement, but soundness is not likely an issue. |
| Toed-out | Hooves and/or legs turn out to the sides. Probably inherited. | Less of a health concern if the entire leg is turned out. See Toed-in. |
| In at the knees | The carpus, or knee, is offset toward the inside of the cannon bone. Probably inherited. | If the horse does not hit himself, this is unlikely to be a problem in the dressage. See Toed-in |
| Over at the knee | Knees bend forward. Possibly inherited. | More a visual distraction than an actual fault. |

| IMPERFECTION | DESCRIPTION | POSSIBLE SIDE EFFECTS AND SOLUTIONS |
|---|---|---|
| Back at the knee | A plumb line drawn from the top of the forearm to the hoof would show a backward arch at the knee. Possibly inherited. | See Toed-in |
| Tied in at the knee | Instead of the cannon bone being parallel throughout its length, it tapers off, narrowing at the back of the knee. Possibly inherited. | Not necessarily a problem in dressage but can predispose a horse to bowed tendons. |
| Long cannon bones | Short cannon bones, also known as hocks low to the ground, are desired. Hocks high off the ground indicate cannon bones that are too long.. Probably inherited | Long cannon bones are considered to be weak. They are blamed for a short stride, especially when combined with a short forearm. Also contributes to a choppy, uncomfortable gait. |
| Cow hocked and sickle-hocked | These are usually found together. Cow hocks can be seen from the rear end of the horse, while sickle hocks slant under the horse and are seen from the side. Probably inherited. | Considered a fault, but many performance horses are uninhibited by this fault. |
| Upright Gaskin | The hind leg of the horse is nearly upright instead of | This can affect the horse's flexibility and |

| IMPERFECTION | DESCRIPTION | POSSIBLE SIDE EFFECTS AND SOLUTIONS |
|---|---|---|
| Gaskin (cont.) | having an angle from the stifle to the hock. Probably inherited. | hinder his attempt to reach under himself. Upright stifles are prone to locking up, which is when the joint pops out of the socket. A powerful hip can compensate for this fault. |

## Body

| | | |
|---|---|---|
| Ewe neck | A dip in the neck in front of the withers. The neck ideally should rise out of the withers. It can be accentuated by overly developed muscles under the neck as in upside-down neck.   While neck shape is likely to be inherited, a ewe neck, or upside-down neck can be exaggerated by poor training and reduced or eliminated by proper training. | Considered a weakness in the topline. Exercise can help to strengthen the neck and make it less of a liability. |
| Neck too long | If the horse can't be divided into even thirds, because the neck portion of the horse is longest, then the neck is too long. Possibly inherited. | A long neck is considered weak, but can be strengthened with exercises and also compensated for with a power ful hip and back. |

| IMPERFECTION | DESCRIPTION | POSSIBLE SIDE EFFECTS AND SOLUTIONS |
|---|---|---|
| Thick throatlatch | The area on the underside of the horse's neck where the head attaches is the throatlatch. If there is no tapering off, if the neck remains a constant line all the way to the head, then the throat latch is heavy.<br><br>Likely inherited, but can be increased by obesity, and decreased using neck sweats. | Most often a problem when the jowls are also thick. The horse may have difficulty breathing when asked to come on the bit. |
| Upside-down neck | Neck bulges out at the bottom.<br><br>Sign of training problems. | Can be helped through exercises. |
| Upright shoulder | Shoulder is at less than 45-degree angle. The angle of the pasterns and the shoulders usually match.<br><br>Likely inherited. | Can be a factor in limiting a horse's reach. Horse may have a short, choppy stride. May be compensated for by a long forearm and free elbow. |
| Back too long | If the horse can't be divided into even thirds because the back portion of the horse is longest, then the back is considered too long.<br><br>Probably inherited. | A possible weakness, but can be compensated for by a muscular loin and hip. |

| IMPERFECTION | DESCRIPTION | POSSIBLE SIDE EFFECTS AND SOLUTIONS |
|---|---|---|
| Short hip/croup | From the point of the hip to the stifle joint. A short croup is apparent if this third of the horse is noticeably shorter than the other two thirds.<br>    Probably inherited. | The bulk of a dressage horse's power comes from his hindquarters. A short croup can be a liability. |
| Elevated hindquarters | When the hip is higher than the withers, the horse has elevated hind-quarters. Though a natural, temporary condition for most young horses, it is often found in Western breeds in adult horses.<br>    Probably inherited. | Considered a liability when training for self-carriage. Horses may have more tendency to travel on the forehand. More serious a problem if combined with a short croup.<br>    A muscular loin and hindquarter can compensate. |
| Roach back | Loin area is elevated higher than either the hips or the withers, and the spine protrudes even when the horse is well fed.<br>    Likely a genetic defect, not always passed on to foals. | Ill fitting saddles can cause a roach-backed horse to buck. Lack of muscling across the loin area is of concern if higher levels of dressage are sought. |

# Chapter Three
## Movement

**M**ovement is more dependable than conformation when judging a young horse's future potential. According to Hilda Gurney, former Olympian, R judge, and sporthorse breeder, "The horse's movement is the proof of its conformation. When the horse is standing still, you can only guess at its conformation. If when a horse stands it has a long back, but when it moves it tracks up and doesn't function like a horse with a long back, then the long back is not a problem. If a horse is built downhill but has uphill movement, then the downhill build is not a problem."

### The Walk

**T**he walk is a four-beat gait. The *USA Equestrian* (formerly the American Horse Show Association and now referred to as USAEq) *Rule Book Art. 1903* describes the walk as "A marching pace in which the footfalls of the horse's feet follow one another in four time, well marked and maintained in all work at the walk." The beats should be clear and even. The rhythm should be 1,2,3,4. An impure or bad walk would have an uneven rhythm like 1,2-3,4. If the legs on the same side move almost laterally on the same beat, the walk is considered irregular.

The walk is the more important of the two gaits judged on the triangle. If the walk is bad, it won't improve. A slight exception to this is in the case of a sluggish horse. The application of aids can improve the impulsion of the walk, but the overall quality of the gait is the same. The walk is an indicator of what the canter will be like; if the walk is good, the canter is likely to be good.

An overstride is highly desired, but at the very least, the horse should track up. Tracking up is when the hind hooves step into or near the prints left by the front hooves. An overstride is when the hind hooves step ahead of the prints left by the front hooves. This indicates a horse's natural inclination to be forward in his movement. Overstride is looked for in the walk and in the extended trot. A horse's walk should at least step into the prints left by the front hooves. The overstride, like every other movement, needs to be balanced. If a horse is tracking over, but his front legs are short-strided, then the movement loses its appeal. All four legs must work evenly, with each reaching out as far as the others.

Another bonus to look for is in the way the horse

moves his body as he walks. Some horses move from their legs and the body quietly follows. This walk, and often the trot, is rather flat and ordinary, although it can be quite smooth to ride. Many Western pleasure horses and hunters have this type of movement. Other horses, frequently Warmbloods, have a desirable characteristic known as *schwung*, which along with an eye catching, self-assured attitude includes when the hips, shoulders, back and tail sway with each step as the entire body is involved with the movement. When the horse moves in this way he is said to be moving through the back. Though this takes more effort on the rider's part to sit, it adds to the beauty and character of the horse's gaits.

A horse with conformation faults may have less-than-attractive movement such as winging or paddling where the hoof and cannon swing out to the side, or knees bowing out to the side with each step. Instead, a horse's legs should move evenly underneath him at all four corners with little noticeable deviation.

## The Trot

The trot is a two-beat gait. *The USAEq Rule Book Art. 1904* describes the trot as, "a pace of two time on alternate diagonal legs (near left fore and right hind leg and vice versa) separated by a moment of suspension."

The rhythm should be 1,2,1,2. Some trots are superficially flashy. The forelegs swing far out with forward motion but the hind legs are not engaged and push out from behind instead of under the horse, limiting the horse's impulsion. The horse needs to track up in the trot, otherwise he is not using his hindquarters properly. If the trot has an even tempo, noticeable suspension and the horse tracks up, that is sufficient for a young horse. The trot can be improved with training.

Huge movement is often what places in in-hand classes, but as one trainer told me, "Olympic horses don't have that extravagant movement. You can't collect all that. Who would want to have to sit all that?"

A flashy trot can be an advantage in-hand, but may not be an advantage later on. Most upper-level movements are canter work and the trot as a piaffe (looks like a collected trot in-place) and passage (an extremely collected trot that

*Though not flashy, this trot will serve the horse well in the lower levels.*

looks like a slow-moving dance) and a collected trot. Extended trot is used in the upper levels, but a good extended trot can be brought out with correct training. Cavalletti can be a good training tool for teaching a horse to extend his trot. A horse with an extravagant trot needs a lot of other qualities to succeed as a dressage horse.

## The Canter

The canter is a three-beat gait. *The USAEq Rule Book Art. 1905* states, " The canter is a pace of three time, where a canter to the right, for instance, the footfalls follow one another as follows: left hind, left diagonal (simultaneously left fore and right hind) right fore, followed by a moment of suspension with all four feet in the air before the next stride begins."

A balanced, cadenced, suspended canter with hooves lightly contacting the ground with each stride is desirable, but young horses can lack balance and are likely to move fast, pounding the ground as they go. This is why the walk is looked at closely to provide clues about the canter. A clear, three beat rhythm is important to observe. Also desirable is a noticeable moment of suspension and a rocking quality to the canter. The horse eventually will have to learn lead changes, and these are easier learned if the horse is naturally balanced.

Judges are quick to notice four-beat canters. This is an impure state of the gait. It frequently can be found in horses previously trained for Western pleasure, because they are asked to move so slowly that they can't continue with a pure canter. Speeding up the horse helps reengage his hindquarters and is usually the remedy.

## Gait Basics

Forward motion is desired in all gaits as this is the basis of impulsion and therefore self-carriage. There is a subtle lift of the horse's frame as he begins a trot or canter. In the canter the legs of the horse will, of course, have both forward and backward motion, but in the canter of a future dressage prospect the legs need to do the bulk of their work tilted toward the front of the horse. The forelegs should be seen to work more in front of the girth area than behind it, while the hind legs come more in front of the hip area. The opposite would be a horse that propels himself forward with his forelegs dragging behind the girth area, and his hind legs not coming very much in front of his hip. This is an indication that the animal is moving heavily on the forehand.

There is a general forward tilt to the movement of a horse's legs when he is using his haunches and a general backward tilt to the leg movement when he is on the forehand. A horse that is naturally inclined to traveling on the forehand will find dressage difficult and will have to work harder to achieve correct movement.

All horses carry most of their weight on the forehand. With all the talk of dressage horses elevating their forehands and carrying their weight on their rear ends, even dressage horses carry more than half their weight on their forehands. The shift between moving on the forehand to on the haunches is only about two percent. The advantage of a horse with natural forward movement is that training and performing will be easier.

*USAEq Rule Book Article 1901* Object and General Principles of Dressage, says, "The object of dressage is the harmonious development of the physique and ability of the horse. As a result it makes the horse calm, supple, loose and flexible, but also confident, attentive and keen thus achieving perfect understanding with his rider ... He responds to the slightest indication of his rider and thereby gives life and spirit to all the rest of his body."

It will take practice, training and talent to reach the above goal. Even Training Level can be a challenge for a rider bringing along a green horse. Starting with a young horse is starting at the very beginning. It takes practice to develop an eye for conformation and movement. Horses well suited for other disciplines may have conformation and movement that is very different from that desired in an upper-level dressage horse, but any healthy horse is a candidate for the lower levels, and many people find that dressage training is helpful no matter what the horse's real career. ❧

# Chapter Four
## Training Techniques

### Early Days, Lasting Impressions

Training should begin the day the foal is born. Imprinting is a method used by some people. Though the true definition is "to fix on the mind or memory", and while there are many ways of doing this, there is a particular method of imprinting that was developed by Dr. Robert Miller. There have been studies done claiming that, in the end, one can't tell the difference between a grown horse that has been imprinted and one that was not. That does not discount imprinting, but it reinforces the fact that there is no one right way to train a horse. Any type of gentle handling a foal receives will make the animal more trusting of humans and easier to handle, therefore safer. Foals that have little or no handling until they are 4 to 6 months old will be difficult at the least. They can be hard to catch, apt to rear, bite or strike once they are caught, and are not likely to be willing to cooperate.

Regardless of technique, if a young horse is to be shown in-hand or under saddle it is imperative that he be

*Any type of gentle handling a foal receives will make him more trusting of humans and easier to handle.*

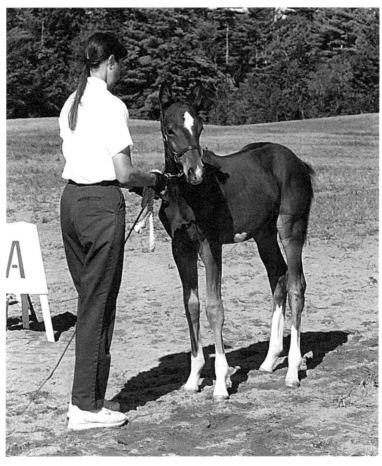

trained and worked with to such an extent that he trusts humans. Horses can be dangerous. A trusting horse is much safer to be around than one that is not trusting.

A foal, no matter how beautiful, how well bred or how great a mover, is not born knowing how to lead, to stand for grooming or to behave with manners. For as many horse trainers as there are, just as many methods of training horses exist. In this chapter we will discuss methods that have been successfully used by professional handlers.

## Safety

There is a danger present when showing sporthorses, or when handling any horse for whatever reason. A warmblood awaiting entry to a class will not necessarily be calm, with his hips askew, standing only on three legs as he rests one hind leg on his toe, neck lowered, ears flopped to the side and lower lip dangling. Such a horse as that would probably not be a danger to anyone, unless something caught his attention and a change in his demeanor transpired. A sporthorse has presence, and along with this presence comes a keen alertness to his surroundings. An alert horse is ready for action. That in itself presents a real potential danger for all humans within spooking distance.

Horses outweigh humans by more than a half-ton, they can outrun and outmaneuver us just as a speedboat can outmaneuver a slow moving manatee. Dealing with horses is a challenge and ours is not a safe sport. Because of this, many states have adopted equine liability laws that include language such as "inherent risks of equine activities." The danger element exists.

The only leverage humans have, besides developing trust with an animal and training him to the best of our abilities, is wits, which on occasion can be dim from lack of sleep, lack of experience or distractions. Don't be lulled into thinking that only beginners get into trouble with horses. Experienced horsepeople can be injured or killed, and often it is due to circumstances beyond their control. In an attempt to avoid disas-

*However calm-natured a horse is, he is capable of presenting danger to any humans near him.*

ter we must use the tools we have available to us, which are common sense, trust and training. If a horse is going to spook but knows better than to invade your space, he will be more likely to choose a direction away from you to spook.

The following training suggestions should be practiced for only short periods of time. For a young horse to become people friendly, it is important that more time is spent rubbing and scratching the foal than training him. Horses become very friendly and come whenever they see people if they can expect to get a thorough scratch on the chest, shoulder or stomach. A horse that only has contact with humans when there is work to do may end up difficult to catch or, at the very least, sour faced when in human company.

A foal should be haltered and taught to lead as early as three days to a week after birth as he is easier and safer to handle when small. Handlers should always wear gloves to prevent rope burn and to give themselves extra gripping ability. In the beginning, two handlers are needed—one to lead the foal's dam as the foal is likely to more or less follow her and one handler is needed to lead the foal.

During the first few sessions, some balking should be expected and should not be punished. Punishment at this early stage can alienate the foal and make him less willing to cooperate. Sometimes a foal can be encouraged to move forward if his handler drapes a rope around his haunches and gives a light tug. Many antics such as, rearing, balking and laying down in defeat are normal. If the foal becomes too agitated, end the session with kind words and patting. The sessions should last only five to 10 minutes and are best ended when the foal is moving forward reasonably.

Horses, like children, learn best if they are not drilled. Try to keep the sessions short and successful. If a youngster does something right, it is best to praise him and end the session immediately. Horses have excellent memories and are creatures of habit, whether good habit or bad. This should be taken advantage of during the training routine. Far more is accomplished by ending a well-done session within the first five minutes rather then by spending 15 minutes in which the horse does two things correctly and three things wrong.

A horse remembers what he did last time and is apt to repeat his performance. A short, well-done session is a valuable training tool in itself.

## Training for the Triangle

After a few weeks, once the foal is following his dam nicely and reliably he needs to be led short distances away from her to teach him to follow his handler's cues.

If the foal balks and can't be coaxed, an assistant handler with a lunge whip is helpful. She can give the foal the incentive needed to move forward. This method is also useful for older horses that were never taught to lead. The assistant with the lunge whip stays on the same side of the horse as the handler. Otherwise she might chase the young horse into the handler. The whip handler needs to take care to be far enough behind the horse not to be reached by the hind hooves. Again, the work should only last a few minutes and end on a good note. At this stage, the goal is only to move the horse forward on command.

When the handler is ready, she clucks to the horse and signals the assistant by raising her left hand at the same time. The moment the handler cues the horse to move forward, the assistant must reinforce that request with a swing from the whip. At first the whip should swing slowly so the reaction of the foal can be determined, and an excessively violent reaction

*This well-mannered and confident Andalusian foal shows the result of patient, correct training.*

can be avoided. The lash of the whip should swing close to the foal's ankles, but not touch him. The foal most likely will spring forward. It needs to be stressed again that the assistant with the whip needs to remain behind the handler and the lash of the whip should swing from the handler's side of the foal to the opposite side, otherwise the foal might inadvertently be directed to run into his handler.

It doesn't take many times before a foal will move at the handler's shoulder at both a walk and a trot at the slightest cue. Work with the young horse should be limited to no more than three times per week and no more than 15 minutes at a time. More than this may sour the foal.

Once the horse is doing walk/trot transitions easily and can stand in the open position for a few minutes a couple of training sessions per month can be sufficient enough to keep the foal consistent, yet fresh. It doesn't do any good to have the horse made to be strictly obedient. He may lose his desire to show himself off and, instead, follow his handler meekly and dully.

## Space

Simple things can be done in a short time to make the young horse safer and easier to handle. While grooming, a foal should be pushed this way and that, as needed. This lets him know he has to move when asked. He should never be allowed to move or fidget into his handler's space. If he does step into her space, the handler must stand her ground and push him away. The handler can move into the horse's space at any time, but the horse must be taught to respect the handler's space at all times. Teaching the horse to move away from pressure will be helpful later on as he is asked to move one leg slightly forward or back while standing up for a judge. This eventually translates into leg yields and half passes once he is going under saddle.

Once the foal responds to being pushed away, teach him to move away when signaled to do so with a whip. First, the horse should be desensitized to the whip by slowly stroking it along both sides until his reaction is calm. Once this is accomplished, hold the lead in one hand and gently, rhythmically and slowly tap the horse's haunches, shoulder, or side with the whip until he takes a step away. Stop the tapping as a reward to him. The handler can get the horse to move forward, back or to step to each side with this method. This is useful when positioning the horse just right for showing, for gaining cooperation during trailer loading or entering a stall and, of course, when asking for various movements once under saddle.

Another way to enforce the space issue is to put the foal on a lead, and get him to stand quietly. Then the handler should walk into the horse's space and then back away. The foal will naturally be inclined to follow, but when he does he must be pushed back into the hoofprints he vacated. The handler must send the message that she can invade the horse's space anytime, but the horse may not invade the handler's space. Horses are very sensitive to the issues of space. By insisting that your space be respected you are telling the horse that you are the herd boss. The herd boss has control of the movements of every horse within the herd. That is the necessary position for a horseperson to be in.

Gaining respect for the whip makes learning turns easier for the horse. Respect for the whip is also useful when leading. Young horses sometimes crowd or turn in front of their handlers. By swinging the butt end of the whip in the handler's left hand like a pendulum, forward and back, the handler points the way she has decided to go. If the horse objects to going that way, he punishes himself by allowing his nose to get in the path of the whip.

## Teaching Turns

Teach the horse to turn by doing small circles, first at a walk and then at a trot. To get a horse to turn away when making the corner, the butt end of the dressage whip is instrumental. To warn the horse of the upcoming change in direction, the handler should give the horse a slight half halt (light pulling back, as if to stop) with the reins or the lead shank if he wears a halter. The handler points toward the direction she intends to take with the butt end of the dressage whip. The handler turns abruptly and marches toward the horse's head with the butt end of the whip pointing the way and her open hand moving toward the horse's eye. The horse should automatically turn away from the whip and the handler. With a few practice sessions, the horse should have a good grasp on turns.

At the trot, it is safer to stop the horse before turning,

and many professional handlers do this. To cue for stops, raise the whip hand straight up to about head level. If the horse responds well to the half halt and turn at the walk, he may do it just as well at the trot. However, the turns at the trot should not be overpracticed or the horse might learn to evade the handler. To trot corners when showing on the triangle, the markers need to be overshot to make broad turns rather than sharp turns. If the majority of practice at home includes stops before turning and slow trot circles, the at-speed turns will remain smooth.

Focusing on a point in the distance, such as a tree or a fence post helps the handler remain on track and not be

*(Left) Using the whip and body language to communicate a turn to the horse. (Right) The horse understands the signal and turns easily.*

gradually pushed off course by the horse. Professional handlers walk with their destination firmly in mind. The horse they are leading may be bouncing and distracted, but invariably he follows the handler's lead. When the handler is sure of her destination the horse is aware of this, as horses are conscious of this subtle language. On the other hand, a horse that knows he can push his handler off course is aware of that too! The one in charge of the direction taken is the one in charge.

Practice for showing on the triangle should be done mainly in straight lines. Some turning should be practiced, but as far as doing the actual triangle pattern, it is recommended that this be practiced sparingly so that the horse is fresh and

*The horse's response to the handler's whip is the result of training before the show or inspection.*

not bored with it at the show.

*Proper preparation at home makes standing the horse in the open position go smoothly at the show.*

The handler should always overshoot the markers of the triangle rather than stop or turn *at* the markers. This is especially true for the profile along the back of the triangle. The judge wants to see the horse's best gait between those mar-kers. Stopping and turning should be done well outside the boundaries of the markers so as not to interfere with the quality of the horse's trot.

A whip handler may accompany the horse's handler at any show or inspection. Between the two handlers, the horse can be

managed and en-couraged to do his best. Experienced handlers can even get an untrained horse to give a good show of himself by using their whips as walls that the horse is not allowed through, and by guiding him in the direction left open for him.

Teaching a horse to stand up in the open position is something that needs some practice. The horse has to learn to move his front and rear legs when asked. If a horse goes into the ring without this practice he will not likely be still and will not get into or stay in the open position easily. With a little practice the horse learns to obey subtle pushes and pulls on the bridle to move his legs as asked. This is another thing that should not be overworked, or it may result in a dull, sub-servient horse.

Another thing a horse should be taught at home is to lower his head when asked. This is useful for grooming, trimming and bridling. More importantly it can take a horse's mind off a distraction and bring his attention back to his handler. Lowering his head is an act of submission. If the horse is taught to be submissive when asked, he often can be calmed down during a disturbing situation.

To achieve this, rhythmically tug downward on the halter until the horse consents to lowering his head. Reward the horse with both praise and by discontinuing the request. With practice the horse will learn to lower his head as soon as he is asked. 🙿

# Chapter Five
## Grooming, Appearance and Presentation

D ress for the handler in the in-hand class used to be strictly black and white. Today some top handlers wear their farm's colors and even prints.

A polo shirt, sometimes with a sweater if the weather is cool, and casual, loose-fitting pants and running shoes are the basic attire.

Jeans are not acceptable, and riding clothes are discouraged. The *Rulebook* stipulates that an exhibitor wearing jeans or other inappropriate attire can be dismissed from the class. However, sometimes even top handlers have been known to show in jeans. As one judge said of the situation, "After splashing in mud for three days, they have nothing left to wear. They can only pack so many pants."

Conservative colors are recommended by both USAEq and USDF because attention must remain on the horse. Distracting prints and clashing colors can interfere with a judge's concentration. At the same time, adherence to originally accepted style can be downright boring especially if there is a lack of attention to detail. Handlers often wear white shirts (baggy and sagging at the waist) and pale pants

*A nicely turned out horse and handler at Dressage at Devon.*

splattered to the hips with mud. This in no way adds to the picture while presenting a beautiful horse. Mud can't be avoided, but medium to dark pants call less attention to it than pale colors do.

Colors that compliment both horse and handler are pleasing to the eye. One well dressed handler, at Devon, wore the traditional white pants and shirt, but he also donned a vest and tie of russet and gold. This did happen to be a muddy day, but he was strikingly put together and the mud splatters were easily overlooked. He walked beside a shining bay, and the pair was truly stunning. Other handlers were nondescript in sloppy fitting white shirts and splattered pants and did not demand a second glance.

If you choose to wear color it should not be over-whelming. A dash here and there can be charming, and create an aesthetically pleasing view. Certain colors of horses go better with some colors than with others. Chestnuts look stunning walking with a handler in a green polo shirt with khaki pants, or a yellow or blue polo shirt with black pants. However they don't look as attractive with shades of pink or red, and are not at their best in most muted colors.

Black horses look good with any color, but look especially nice with black and white, yellow, red, pink or green. Bays look nice with sharp colors like royal blue, red or Kelly green, and a nice blend can be made with many shades of tan. Greys look best with muted colors such as teal, rose or blue, however they also look good with sharp colors like red, green and black. A grey horse would look average in shades of brown or tan.

To gain insight on colors that look best together look at studies done on women's fashion, or go to a local Western show and look at the outfits. The Western riders, while gaudy compared to the riders in the English disciplines, put a great deal of effort into matching their outfits with their horses.

## To Shave or Not to Shave?

European horses' faces are kept natural, that is, unshaven. American show horses, regardless of discipline, are often clean-shaven from fetlock to ear tip. Sporthorses sometimes have their muzzles and eye whiskers left intact.

Whiskers and other body hair serve a specific purpose for the horse. Whiskers increase a horse's sensitivity to his immediate surroundings and are useful to animals turned out at night. Ear hair keeps insects and dust from irritating the inside of the horse's ears. Rather than shaving out the ear completely, trim any stray hairs flush with the surface of the ear. Clearing out the ear hair out entirely can make a large, stately warmblood less attractive as the dark cavity can draw attention to a coarse set of ears. A light surface trim retains the ear's protective hair yet at the same time gives a neat, cared-for appearance. To do this light trim gently fold the ear closed lengthwise and trim any protruding hairs.

Feathers, the long hair at the horse's fetlock, have the purpose of detouring rainwater away from the heels, preventing such maladies as mudfever, also known as scratches. Some breeds should have their feathers intact, such as Haflingers and Friesians. Other breeds such as Thoroughbreds, Appaloosas and Quarter Horses have such scant feathering that no trimming is needed in most individuals. For those with unruly feathering, "sculpting" can easily be done to neaten the appearance. If inexperienced in using clippers, practice weeks ahead of a show so any mistakes have time to grow in. Shaving against the grain of the hair is easiest at first,

*A good braiding job and neatly trimmed face and ears, makes a nice impression.*

but downward and upward strokes can be combined once experience has set in. Practice is the only thing between a neat clipping job and unsightly gouges in the hair along the leg.

However, a neat trimming job can also be done using a razor and scissors. Scissors can get the bridle path fairly low, and then the razor can make it neat and flat. Scissors can sculpt feathers and the hairs around the coronet band, while razors mow down whiskers. Clippers are noisy and often frighten or annoy horses and they need constant maintenance and cleaning, but they are fast.

Various methods can be used for getting horses to tolerate clipping. Some are extreme, such as tranquilizing, which, if done too close to the show, can put one in violation of show rules. Twitches are often used. In the end patience is the tool that gives the best results for encouraging good behavior in future trimming. Horses that are gradually introduced to the noise and feel of clipping and trimming can get to the point where they will stand quietly for all of it.

To achieve this the handler must first accustom the animal to grooming and hoof trimming. When he is behaving and well mannered for these tasks, introducing clipping won't be as traumatic. One way to help the horse get used to clipper noise is to turn on the clippers so that the hum can be heard in the background as the horse is groomed. Each day, bring the noise closer to the horse, until he will tolerate the sound next to him. First touch the horse with the clippers off, and then gradually work up to actual clipping. The main point is trust. An animal that trusts his handler will more readily accept something new than one that has been brought in from the pasture, trusting only his fellow herd members.

## Manes and Tails

Dressage horses under saddle often have their manes braided, and tails banged and shaved or pulled along the sides.

In-hand horses certainly look nice shiny from grooming, braided, with tails banged , but all that is really necessary for the show ring is that the young horse be clean and brushed. Many young horses come to the show ring straight from the pasture. Their owners are breeders and have busy lives revolving around the farm. Their interest in showing is only to show the world what they have created. The coats on these young horses are sometimes between sheddings and are pock-marked from bites and kicks and dull from the sun. These horses are judged on their ability, not on their grooming. A horse's mind is valuable. To develop a good mind, a young horse needs the freedom of a pasture and the companionship of other equines. The need for this development of mind surpasses any reason to show.

## Braids

If a horse has been handled enough to tolerate braiding there are several options: button braids, French braids, hunter braids, knob style braids, Continental (also known as macrame) and scalloped braids are all found in the dressage ring. The forelock is either braided or left natural depending on the owner's desire and the horse's appearance.

Knob-style braids numbering between 20–25 and sometimes wrapped with white tape are the most often seen. French braids, scalloped braids and Continental braids are all useful for longer manes that are often common for Andalusians, Arabians, Friesians, Haflingers, Morgans, etc. Knob braids are made in a way similar to Hunter braids (see description on page 104) but when they are tied up the braid is pushed above the crest of the horse's neck. The raised portion is decorated with white tape.

Another style is button braids. These are secure braids that are useful if one needs to have the braids stay in over a few days of showing, as some busy professionals like Hilda

*A lovely example of a button braid.*

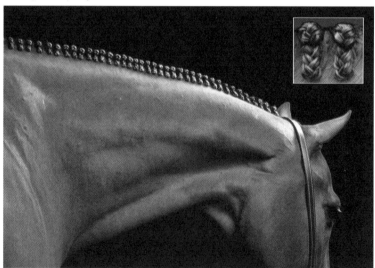

Gurney does. They are less likely to look unsightly if they are not redone daily than are the other styles of braids, and they are also good for a horse with a longer mane. They are sewn in with thick thread. A regular braid is made with thread braided into it in the same way as yarn is. The end of the braid is brought under the crest, and the folded end (that had previously been the middle) is brought under the crest and sewn in. The base of the button is then wrapped by crossing the two ends of thread and tied.

Scalloped braids are a lovely option for a long mane. First, regular braids are made with yarn braided into them. Beginning by the ears, each braid is then passed under the braid next to it and pulled with a latch hook up into the braid beyond that. The thread or yarn is crossed under that braid and pulled

*Continental or macrame braid.*

back up with one piece on each side and then tied. This is repeated until the end. The last braid is brought up in hunter-braid fashion and the previous two braids are tied under it.

Continental braiding is very becoming. It is one of the easiest braiding styles to do. The beginning is similar to Western banding, except that the rubber bands are not tight against the crest. Along the horse's neck make equal "pony-tails." Divide each ponytail in half and use those halves to make another row of ponytails under the first set. This is repeated several times. The two or so inches of manes left at the end of the mane remains loose. White tape can be used to cover the rubber bands.

*The Andalusian Kimona sports a French braid. This type of braid works well on different types of necks; compare with the horse on the next page.*

French braiding is difficult and is more likely to come loose than are other types of braids. It is done in a way similar to that of tails, except that new strands can only be added from one side. The braid can be ended with a hunter-style braid.

Foals sometimes have manes that are too short to braid, and some young horses are too unruly to braid. However, if braiding can be managed it is a good idea as it is considered to be a compliment to the judge.

## Tails

Tails are usually banged, which means the natural tip at the bottom is cut off, making the bottom of the tail

*Aram sports a French braid.*

straight and flat (see the photo on page 78). A long, full tail in a dressage horse is desirable. Judges can tell something about the elasticity of a gait by the swing of a tail. A short tail won't have this telltale swing, but a too long tail might appear slow moving and give a lazy look to the gaits.

The sides of the tail near the dock are shaved or pulled so the hair lies flat in the tail grove. If a horse has a second career, such as a hunter, the sides of the tail should be left long so it can be braided. In this case, the dock of the tail can be dampened with water and wrapped prior to the show to help keep the hairs lying flat against the dock. However, the wrap must be taken off before entering the class.

Sometimes a tail suffers damage from stablemates or foals and is ragged from missing hair. One way chewing damage from other horses can be prevented is by dousing the endangered tail in hot pepper sauce.

## A Shiny Coat

Brushing is the main way to bring out the shine in a horse's coat. Wash the dirt from all the brushes daily and always use a clean brush to groom the horse. A shine on the horse's coat is desirable. Keeping young horses in stalls is not. A judge will not lower the score of a young horse because his coat is sun bleached, but as the horse ages more attention to grooming is expected. The sun is the biggest culprit to ruining the horse's natural shine. Particularly in the summer, horses can be kept up in stalls during daylight hours and turned out to graze at night.

Supplements are often fed to horses to enhance their coats. Many top farms have their own favorites. The main ingredients in most of those supplements are fatty acids, vitamin E, or a combination of both. Bathing very often takes the shine out of the coat. To avoid this, bathe only the dirty areas of the horse and try to keep him clean by brushing, blanketing and stall cleaning. If possible, bathe the day before a show. Some shampoos are less drying than others. Look for one of those when a bath is needed.

Regular vacuuming can keep a coat clean without compromising the shine. As with clippers, the vacuum needs to be introduced slowly and patiently. Allow the horse to become accustomed to the noise before approaching him.

## Bridles and Halters

Very young foals being shown with their dams are sometimes shown free but are more usually shown in a halter. Weanlings are shown in a leather halter. Yearlings may be shown in a bridle, but are most often shown in a halter. The deciding factor lies with the owner and handler. They must determine if the young horse is experienced enough to be well behaved in a bridle. If the horse is attending his first show or is highly excitable, a halter is a better choice as the handler can then avoid having to yank on a youngster's tender mouth with the bit.

According to the *USAEq Rule Book*, 2-year-old horses must be shown in a bridle. They need to have experience wearing one ahead of show time or they will gnaw and wretch their mouths unattractively during the class. A horse can be taught from the beginning to accept a bridle willingly.

*(Top) Yearlings may be shown in a bridle, but many are shown in a halter. (Bottom) A well-turned-out youngster with an elegant headstall and beautiful grooming.*

Most novices try to put on a bridle on by grasping the top of the headstall in one hand and raising that hand uselessly in the air near the horse's ears while trying to jam the bit in the horse's mouth with the other. Not only does the person not have any control, it encourages the horse to develop bad habits because avoidance and head throwing are made easier for him.

For better control, the headstall should be grasped with one hand a few inches above the bit and that hand placed on top of the horse's nose. The other hand should hold the bit and be under the horse's mouth and chin. Pressing a finger into the corner of the horse's mouth where there are no teeth will gently force the horse's mouth open. The bit should be put in as he opens his mouth and then the headstall brought up to the ears.

The reins should be draped over the horse's neck and not left dragging on the ground to be stepped on and broken.

The first time a horse wears a bridle, the bit shouldn't be left in for more than 15-20 minutes. After that, a half an hour a day until the horse has excepted its presence will suffice. Some people leave the bit in all day the first time a horse has it in to get him used to it quickly. This is not kind. A slower introduction is good training and will not cause the horse undue stress.

If the horse has an attractive head, the noseband can be omitted. Try the bridle on with and without the noseband to determine what way is most attractive on your horse.

Bridles come in many styles and sizes. Coarse heads look better in thick bridles trimmed in white to break up the lines of the horse's face. A pretty head can be lovely in the thick, white trimmed bridle, too, but a thin, rolled style would be elegant, especially if the horse has attractive markings like an hourglass-shaped blaze or a diamond-shaped star.

*(Top) It's better not to use a halter on a small foal if it's not used to wearing one. Otherwise it will buck and not show his gaits. (Bottom) The handler looks back to check on the location of the foal being shown free.*

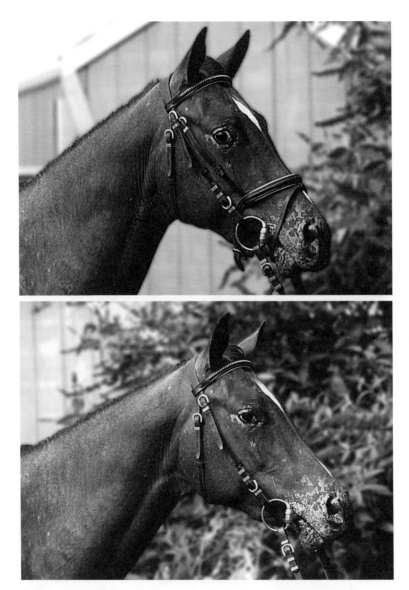

*The presence or absence of a noseband can change the way a horse's head looks.*

Fitting the bridle correctly is necessary for the horse to be comfortable. If he is not comfortable he will fidget rather than stand placidly. The bit, which should be a mild snaffle such as a hollow-mouth eggbutt, will push in at the corners of the horse's mouth if it is too narrow, and this pinches the horse's mouth. A bit that is too wide (more than one-half inch sticking out from each side) will hang too low in the horse's mouth and will cause excessive worrying with the bit.

*One method of attaching a chain to a bridle.*

When the bit is resting in the horse's mouth it should gently pull upward until a wrinkle or two can be seen at the corners of his mouth. When the reins are pulled back, the cheekpieces should not gape; this is a sign the bridle is too loose. If a noseband is used, it should be fastened under the cheek straps. Be sure to put all strap ends in their keepers for a neat, finished appearance.

Reins are usually used in in-hand classes, but a lead shank with a chain can be substituted. The handler's right hand holds the reins or lead shank close to the horse's mouth to guide his direction. In the handler's left hand the remaining length is held in such a way that merely opening the hand frees the reins. They should never be wrapped around the handler's hand so she won't be dragged should the horse attempt to break away.

## Attaching a Chain

There are several ways to attach the chain of a lead rope. For a mild-mannered horse, running it through the bottom loop of the halter hooking it to itself is enough. This does not hurt the horse's face in any way, but does give a strong vibration when jerked. This method is gentle enough to use on foals. For a horse that requires a stronger aid, the chain can be run through the openings on each side of the halter either under the chin, or over the nose and attached to itself. A harsh jerk should be avoided, especially when the chain is under the chin, as it would be a severe punishment. Most horses respond easily to slight tugs with the chain woven through the halter this way. The halter should be loose enough that the chain rests loosely under the horse's chin. It should not be tight, or the horse will be punished the entire time the chain is on the halter.

The method of running a chain from one cheek-ring of a halter, over the horse's nose, and hooked to opposite cheek-ring is of medium severity and is a popular method with Western halter horse owners. However, unless the halter is fit snuggly to the horse's face, the chain can pull the halter into the horse's eye. 🙿

# Chapter Six
## Showing On the Triangle

T he USDF offers a variety of in-hand classes including an annual Breeders Championship series for both young horses (3 and under) and mature horses (4 and older). The series covers eight territories, similar to the regional championships. The purpose of these classes is to promote sporthorse breeding in America.

Each fall, Dressage at Devon, in Devon, Pennsylvania holds many individual breed classes that increase in the variety of breeds and number of entries each year. In addition, many schooling shows and multi-event local shows offer in-hand sporthorse classes. There are classes for weanlings, yearlings, 2-year-olds, 3-year-olds, and 4-year-olds of each sex. There are classes in which all sexes and ages and sometimes breeds are combined. Many breed associations hold inspections for breeding animals. To participate in any of these, a working knowledge of what is expected on the triangle is necessary. The score sheets for USDF Dressage Sport Horse classes are given at the end of this chapter. You should study them ahead of time to know what is expected of competitors and how you will be judged.

*The smaller triangle is done at the walk. The larger triangle is done at the trot. The point where they both meet is the beginning and where the horse is stood up in the open position. The points of the triangle are usually marked with beautiful flowers. The first and third sides are where the judge is looking for straightness and purity of gaits. It is important to go a little slower to insure straightness. The second side of the triangle, referred to as "the back" is where the horse should be most encouraged to show off his gaits. More speed is desired there.*

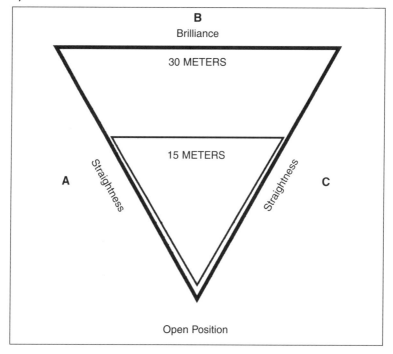

A horse shown on the triangle as a sporthorse (geldings and mares not currently pregnant or with a foal by the side) is judged 30 percent on conformation, 30 percent on the walk, 30 percent on the trot and 10 percent on general impression, which includes impulsion, expression and manners. If the horse is shown in a breeding class (mares and stallions only) they are judged 25 percent on the walk, 25 percent on the trot, 40 percent conformation and 10 percent general impression.

The triangle can be marked out using anything from orange or white cones to fancy potted plants depending on

*The triangle at Devon.*

whether it is a schooling show or an approved USDF event. There are actually two triangles in one, a large and a small. They share the same starting point and most of two sides. The small (inner) triangle is 15 meters on each side. The walk is displayed along the triangle's perimeter. The larger triangle measures 30 meters on each side and is used to show the trot.

A show's management has a choice between two different shaped triangles to use. The one most commonly used is the equilateral triangle previously mentioned. The other is one triangle measuring 30x40x30 meters. The walk and trot are completed on this without dividing it into two.

A good whip handler makes a valuable assistant in presenting the horse in-hand and everyone is allowed one

*The open position is usually the judge's first look.*

assistant. Having one may mean the difference between mediocre and spectacular gaits from the horse.

The open position may be the first thing required of a horse. However, this is entirely up to the judge. The open position is where the front and rear legs of the horse on the side that faces the judge are farther apart than the front and rear legs on the opposite side. All legs should be seen with none hiding behind another. The farthest open legs should be almost directly under the corners of the horse. The hind leg sometimes extends out from the corner, slightly beyond the point of the buttock while the foreleg is directly under the shoulder.

Most judges ask for the open position first, but allow anxious horses to move on to do the walk and trot, and standing them up last. Some judges want to see the open position at both the beginning and the end of the triangle. The decision is theirs.

## Let the Class Begin

The class begins with the exhibitor walking the horse to the first point of the triangle. This is where the horse is stood up for the judge in the open position. The horse is opened to the side facing the judge, which is usually the left side. As the judge walks around the horse, the exhibitor should open the other side.

Novice handlers often are nervous when in close proximity to a judge. Be polite if spoken to and, at least outwardly, try to remain as calm as possible. A nervous handler, through her own fidgeting, often makes a poor showing. The only cure for this is experience. There are classes designated for novice handlers. In these classes, the pressure is less and the judges are understanding and encouraging. Many judges are open to answering questions and are willing to offer advice. Taking advantage of these classes can only improve a handler's ability and therefore improve her relationship with her horse.

When the judge indicates that she is finished evaluating the horse's conformation, the horse proceeds along the small triangle at a walk. The handler must use a brisk, ground-covering walk and encourage the horse to do the same. Moving

*As the judge walks around the horse, the handler should always move to the opposite side.*

in straight lines from one marker to the next is imperative for the judge to determine the quality of the gait. If the horse refuses to be straight and instead spins and wobbles around the arena, the judge may ask the handler to try again to get straight movement from the animal. The walk is finished when the first triangle is completed.

Be sure your turn at the point of the triangle is completed and the horse is straight before asking for the trot. It is important to keep the trot reasonably slow on sides A and C. At these angles the judge is looking for soundness, straightness and rhythm. If the handler speeds along all three sides of the triangle, momentum can be lost at the all- important side B, where the profile is presented and the horse has the opportunity to impress the judge with his extension and suspension, and straightness can be sacrificed at A and C.

On this B side of the triangle,

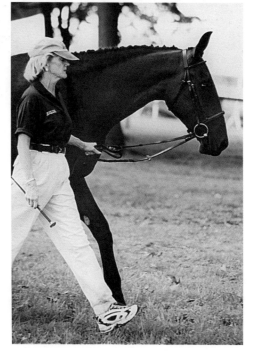

*The handler uses a brisk, ground-covering walk with this Cleveland Bay. Note the length of rein, which allows the horse the freedom to move.*

speed is important, however, it's the handler's speed that must be fast. A large warmblood's brisk trot is not a high-speed gait for a horse, but it is a challenge for some humans to keep up with and not hinder the horse's movement. With horses that have shorter strides, American breeds in particular, asking for too much speed from the horse will cause him to tilt onto his forehand, flattening out his trot. Practice with your horse and an observer to get an idea of the speed, both yours and the horse's, that makes your horse look his best. If the handler can match her stride with that of the

*This very competent, calm-looking pair begin to show the walk.*

horse the view for the judge will be unimpeded by out of sequence leg movements.

Once the horse has completed trotting the triangle, the handler should proceed to set the horse up again in the open position again unless dismissed by the judge. A dismissal at this point has nothing to do with the judge's opin-

*(Below, top) The handler should match her "gait" with the horse's. Note the professional appearance—no blue jeans! (Below, bottom) Matching footfalls with the horse's strides. This is professional handler Willie Arts.*

ion of your horse, but merely indicates that the judge has had sufficient time to evaluate your horse's conformation and does not require a second viewing. A repeat of the open position usually is only asked for if the horse had trouble standing still the first time. However, the handler should always offer to stand the horse up a second time.

*The handler's responsibility is to show the horse off to the judge as this handler does with his Andalusian stallion.*

Throughout the class the judge is looking for quality of gaits, looking to see if the horse moves through the back, and is even looking for elusive signs of personality: Will this horse be proud and have that extra spark in his later years as a Grand Prix horse?

The handler's responsibility is to encourage the horse to show himself off. A handler should be able to proceed with purpose and determination throughout the triangle with the horse coming along easily as part of a unit, and yet with his individuality unhindered.

Novice handlers tend to hang on the horse's head at the walk, trot and when standing the horse up. This trait throws off the horse's balance and ruins his carriage. To get

*Judging from the ribbon, this handler has been successful at showing of his horse's beautiful trot!*

the best out of the horse, the horse needs to respect the handler's space, and needs to move at the handler's shoulder. The handler needs to have enough confidence to guide the horse with light contact.

## Presentation for Breed Inspections

While there are no points counting toward year-end awards and no trophies, inspection is an important issue for breeders. They want their horse not only to pass well enough to be included in the breed's studbook, but want the horse to prove his quality by receiving a high score. A horse should look his best at a breed show, but this is even more

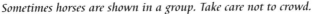

*Sometimes horses are shown in a group. Take care not to crowd.*

important at an inspection. The scores a horse receives will become part of his permanent record. Time and effort should be put into his grooming and condition months in advance. The horse's mane should be neatly braided, and he should wear a bridle that flatters his head.

Horses presented for inspection are shown in much the same way as those shown at breed shows. Each breed association has special requirements  or traditions, so it is important to know ahead of time what will be expected.

One additional requirement might be for all the horses being inspected to circle the inspectors at a walk. Keep plenty of distance between the horses as crowding can easily turn into kicking. ❧

## USDF Dressage Sport Horse Prospects (In-Hand)

### Individual Scoresheet

**NO.**

| Specifications | Directive Ideas | Points | Coefficient | Total | Comments |
|---|---|---|---|---|---|
| **Conformation:** *Criteria:* The quality & correctness of: head, neck, saddle position, shoulder, frame, back, forehand, hindquarters, angulation & formation of legs and joints. | Predisposition to unsoundness or limitations in quality of movement, caused by weaknesses or conformation faults, potential for trainability and performance. Emphasis on function, not fashion. Blemishes are not to count unless resulting from conformation faults. Good harmonious conformation suitable for dressage performance. | | x3.0 or 30% | | |
| **Movement:** **Walk:** *Criteria:* Four even beats, straight & even strides, correctly aligned steps, articulation of joints, freedom of shoulders & haunches, balance, elastic & swinging back, overstep, reach, ground-covering with marching quality. | Purity & Quality (judged mainly in profile), Correctness (judged mainly coming to & going from judge). | | x3.0 or 30% | | |
| **Trot:** *Criteria:* Two even beats, straight & even strides, correctly aligned steps, articulation of joints, freedom of shoulders & haunches, balance, elasticity, swinging back, natural engagement & impulsion from hindquarters, suspension, power from upward thrust & roundness. | Purity & Quality (judged mainly in profile), Correctness (judged mainly coming to & going from judge). Movement should be big, light & springy. | | x3.0 or 30% | | |
| **General Impression:** *Criteria:* Includes impulsion, balance, harmony & development related to age & typiness. Alert, expressive & well-mannered. | Riding horse type. | | x1.0 or 10% | | |

(Decimals may be used in Scoring)

**Total Adjusted Points** _____ (100 points possible)

**Further Remarks:**                    **Percentage** _____ **Entry No.** _____

Judge's Signature(s) _____

*USDF Dressage Sport Horse Prospects Score Sheet. © 1997 USDF. Used by the kind permission of the USDF, Inc.*

## Individual Group Scoresheet

*Note: The entire group is considered one entry and is given one total/combined score in each category. Only one number card per group.*

**NO.**

The following are considered Group classes. In giving each score, the following relative weights are given to each portion of the group:
*(Groups should consist of 2 or no more than 3 offspring/get)*

☐ Broodmare & Foal, Dam & Produce - 50% mare & 50% offspring
☐ Sire & Get - 50% stallion & 50% get
☐ Produce of Dam, Get of Sire, Breeder's Group - equal weight for each offspring
☐ Family Class - 50% overall quality & 50% improvement in successive breedings

| Specifications | Directive Ideas | Points Coefficient | Total | Comments |
|---|---|---|---|---|
| **Conformation:** *Criteria:* The quality & correctness of: head, neck, saddle position, shoulder, frame, back, forehand, hindquarters, angulation & formation of legs and joints. | Substance, condition, durability, heritable faults which affect soundness, trainability or breeding. Emphasis on function, not fashion. Penalize transmissible weaknesses, unsoundnesses or limitations in quality of movement. Blemishes are not to count unless resulting from conformation faults. Good harmonious conformation suitable for producing dressage performers. | x 4.0 or 40% | | |
| **Movement:** **Walk:** *Criteria:* Four even beats, straight & even strides, correctly aligned steps, articulation of joints, freedom of shoulders & haunches, balance, elastic & swinging back, overstep, reach, ground-covering with marching quality. | Purity & Quality (judged mainly in profile), Correctness (judged mainly coming to & going from judge). | x 2.5 or 25% | | |
| **Trot:** *Criteria:* Two even beats, straight & even strides, correctly aligned steps, articulation of joints, freedom of shoulders & haunches, balance, elasticity, swinging back, natural engagement & impulsion from hindquarters, suspension, power from upward thrust & roundness. | Purity & Quality (judged mainly in profile), Correctness (judged mainly coming to & going from judge). Movement should be big, light & springy. | x 2.5 or 25% | | |
| **General Impression:** *Criteria:* Includes masculinity (stallion) & femininity (mare), development related to age, harmony & typiness. Alert, expressive & well-mannered. Improvement in successive generations of family. | Uniformity of quality and overall quality of the group. Clear sex type in breeding stock. | x 1.0 or 10% | | |

(Decimals may be used in Scoring)

**Further Remarks:**

**Total Adjusted Points** _____ (100 points possible)

**Percentage** _____ **Entry No.** _____

USDF©1997

**Judge's Signature(s)** _____

---

*USDF Dressage Sport Horse Group Class Score Sheet. © 1997 USDF. Used by the kind permission of the USDF, Inc.*

# USDF Dressage Sport Horse Breeding Stock (In-Hand)

*Individual Scoresheet*

**NO.**

| Specifications | Directive Ideas | Points | Coefficient | Total | Comments |
|---|---|---|---|---|---|
| **Conformation:**<br>*Criteria:*<br>The quality & correctness of: head, neck, saddle position, shoulder, frame, back, forehand, hindquarters, angulation & formation of legs and joints. | Substance, condition, durability, heritable faults which affect soundness, trainability or breeding. Emphasis on function, not fashion. Penalize transmissible weaknesses, unsoundnesses or limitations in quality of movement. Blemishes are not to count unless resulting from conformation faults. Good harmonious conformation suitable for producing dressage performers. | | x4.0 or 40% | | |
| **Movement:**<br>**Walk:**<br>*Criteria:*<br>Four even beats, straight & even strides, correctly aligned steps, articulation of joints, freedom of shoulders & haunches, balance, elastic & swinging back, overstep, reach, ground-covering with marching quality. | Purity & Quality (judged mainly in profile), Correctness (judged mainly coming to & going from judge). | | x2.5 or 25% | | |
| **Trot:**<br>*Criteria:*<br>Two even beats, straight & even strides, correctly aligned steps, articulation of joints, freedom of shoulders & haunches, balance, elasticity, swinging back, natural engagement & impulsion from hindquarters, suspension, power from upward thrust & roundness. | Purity & Quality (judged mainly in profile), Correctness (judged mainly coming to & going from judge). Movement should be big, light & springy. | | x2.5 or 25% | | |
| **General Impression:**<br>*Criteria:*<br>Includes masculinity (stallion) & femininity (mare), development related to age, harmony & typiness. Alert, expressive & well-mannered. | Breeding horse type. | | x1.0 or 10% | | |

(Decimals may be used in Scoring)

**Total Adjusted Points** _____ (100 points possible)

**Further Remarks:**

**Percentage** _____ **Entry No.**_____

USDF©1997

Judge's Signature(s)_____

---

*USDF Dressage Sport Breeding Stock Score Sheet. © 1997 USDF. Used by the kind permission of the USDF, Inc.*

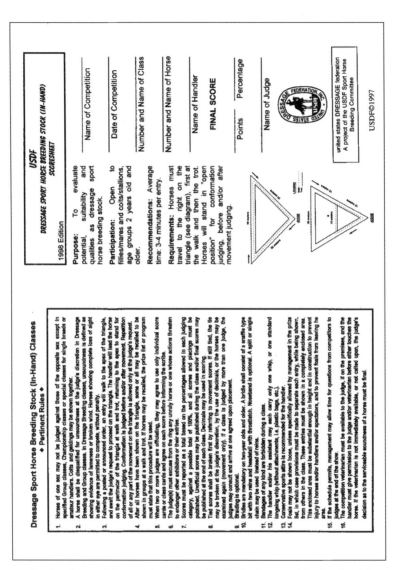

*Back side of one of the test sheets: Read both the front and back side of the test sheets as they contain important information you must know ahead of time. © 1997 USDF. Used by the kind permission of the USDF, Inc.*

# Chapter Seven
## The Next Step: Materiale and Suitability Classes

At Dressage at Devon 2000 materiale classes were held for the first time in the United States. Materiale classes are the next step for a horse to take, between showing in-hand and under saddle competition. In these classes horses ages 3 through 5 are shown under saddle with others of the same age and sex both ways at the walk, trot and canter, and then stripped of the saddle and judged on conformation while standing. The 3-year-old horses are not expected to lengthen stride at this point, but it may be asked of 4 and 5 year-olds. For safety reasons, no more than six horses are asked to canter at one time.

In Suitability for Dressage classes the horse must be under 7 years old and cannot have competed above First Level.

The under-saddle classes are for 3 and 4 year-old horses and are divided by age and sex. In these classes the horse is shown at the walk, trot and canter, but is not usually stripped of his saddle to be judged for conformation, though it is the judge's option to ask this. There is usually no score given in either under saddle or suitability, only placings.

In the under-saddle classes the entries must have been shown in an in-hand class offered that day.

In all of these under-saddle classes, the quality of the

*Unsaddling in the materiale class.*

horse's three gaits are judged, as is the horse's conformation as it relates to function. As with in-hand classes, 10 percent of the score is based on general impression, which includes manners. Manners are a definite plus in any class, but straying from good manners may not necessarily lose one the class. A horse may or may not be penalized for unruly behavior such as bucking. Black and white rules serve as guidelines for judging, but these rules are to be interpreted by individuals and there is no way

*A contestant in the first materiale class held in the United States at Dressage at Devon in 2000.*

**Individual Scoresheet**

NO.

| Specifications | Directive Ideas | Points | Coefficient | Total | Comments |
|---|---|---|---|---|---|
| **Conformation:**<br>*Criteria:*<br>The quality & correctness of: head, neck, saddle position, shoulder, frame, back, forehand, hindquarters, angulation & formation of legs and joints. | Predisposition to unsoundness, or limitations in quality of movement, caused by weaknesses or conformation faults, potential for trainability and performance. Emphasis on function, not fashion. Blemishes are not to count unless resulting from conformation faults. Good harmonious conformation suitable for dressage performance. | | x3.0<br>or<br>30% | | |
| **Movement:**<br>**Walk:**<br>*Criteria:*<br>Four even beats, straight & even strides, correctly aligned steps, articulation of joints, freedom of shoulders & haunches, balance, elastic & swinging back, overstep, reach, ground-covering with marching quality. | Purity & Quality (judged mainly in profile), Correctness (judged mainly coming to & going from judge). | | x2.0<br>or<br>20% | | |
| **Trot:**<br>*Criteria:*<br>Two even beats, straight & even strides, correctly aligned steps, articulation of joints, freedom of shoulders & haunches, balance, elasticity, swinging back, natural engagement & impulsion from hindquarters, suspension, power from upward thrust & roundness. | Purity & Quality (judged mainly in profile), Correctness (judged mainly coming to & going from judge). Movement should be big, light & springy. | | x2.0<br>or<br>20% | | |
| **Canter:**<br>*Criteria:*<br>Three even beats, straight & even strides, correctly aligned steps, articulation of joints, freedom of shoulders & haunches, balance, elasticity, swinging back, natural engagement & impulsion from hindquarters, suspension, power from upward thrust, roundness, & "uphill" strides. | Purity & Quality (judged mainly in profile), Correctness (judged mainly coming to & going from judge). Movement should be big, light & springy. | | x2.0<br>or<br>20% | | |
| **General Impression:**<br>*Criteria:*<br>Includes impulsion, balance & rideability. Alert, expressive & well-mannered. | Riding horse type. | | x1.0<br>or<br>10% | | |

(Decimals may be used in Scoring)

**Further Remarks:**  **Total Adjusted Points** _____ (100 points possible)

**Percentage** _____ **Entry No.** _____

USDF©1997  Judge's Signature(s)_____

*USDF Dressage Sport Horse Prospects (Under Saddle) test sheet front. © 1997 USDF. Used by the kind permission of the USDF, Inc.*

## Dressage Sport Horse Prospects (Under Saddle)
### ◆ Pertinent Rules ◆

1. Horses entered in Dressage/Sport Horse Under Saddle classes must also have been entered and judged in at least one of the in-hand or group classes. Classes for the same sex may be combined at the discretion of the management.

2. A horse shall be disqualified for unsoundness. In Dressage Sport Horse Under Saddle classes, unsoundness is defined as showing evidence of lameness. Horses showing complete loss of sight in either eye are permitted to compete, without penalty.

3. When two or more judges are officiating, they may agree to use only individual score cards or class cards and agree on each score before informing the scribe.

4. Depending on local conditions, under saddle classes may be divided at the judge's discretion.

5. The judge(s) must excuse from the ring any unruly horse or one whose actions threaten to endanger other exhibitors or their entries.

6. Scores must be reported as a total based on the percentages allowed in each judging category, against a possible total of 100%, and all scores and placings must be published. Unofficial scores may be published during the class and/or final scores may be published at the end of each class. Decimals may be used in scoring.

7. Tied scores shall be broken first by referring to movement scores. If still tied, the tie may be broken at the judge's discretion, by the use of decimals, or the horses may be examined again (movement only). If a class is judged by more than one judge, the judges may consult and arrive at one agreed upon placement.

8. Horses may be placed in under saddle classes with no actual scores awarded.

9. Braiding is optional.

10. In Under Saddle classes, Dress must conform to Art. 1920, and Saddlery and Equipment must conform to Art. 1921, except that all horses are required to compete in a snaffle pictured in Rule XIX, Chapter 1, Figure 1A.

11. Bandages of any kind are forbidden during a class.

12. The handler and/or his assistant may each carry only one whip, or one standard longeing whip (without attachments, i.e. plastic bags, etc.).

13. If the schedule permits, management may allow time for questions from competitors to judges at the end of the show.

14. The competition veterinarian must be available to the judge, if on the premises, and the handler must give permission to the judge and/or veterinarian before either touches the horse. If the veterinarian is not immediately available, or not called upon, the judge's decision as to the serviceable soundness of a horse must be final.

---

## USDF
### DRESSAGE SPORT HORSE PROSPECTS (UNDER SADDLE)
### INDIVIDUAL SCORESHEET
1998 Edition

**Purpose:** To evaluate potential, suitability and qualifies as a dressage sport horse (or performance horse).

**Participation:** Open to colts/stallions and geldings ages 3 years old and older.

**Recommendations:** Average time: 10-30 minutes per class.

**Requirements:** Horses will be asked to move at the walk, trot and canter in both directions of the ring. If conformation is to be judged, horses may be asked to be untacked for inspection, or horses may be judged while standing in line under tack and rider.

**Note:** This scoresheet is designed for use for under saddle classes with fewer than 6-8 entries. A Dressage Sport Horse Under Saddle Class scoresheet is available for use with larger classes, where it is not practical to return an individual scoresheet to each entry, or where horses will be placed, with no actual scores awarded.

Name of Competition

Date of Competition

Number and Name of Class

Number and Name of Horse

Name of Handler

**FINAL SCORE**

Points          Percentage

Name of Judge

united states DRESSAGE federation
A project of the USDF Sport Horse Breeding Committee

USDFR©1997

---

*USDF Dressage Sport Horse Prospects (Under Saddle) test sheet back. © 1997 USDF. Used by the kind permission of the USDF, Inc.*

for the judging to be black and white. The rules are a framework and are only brought to life by human interpretation of the various circumstances that make up a horse show.

In the words of Janet Brown, USA Equestrian "S" judge and "R" Sporthorse breeding judge, "There are too many variables in judging: the quality of the horse, the type of resistance. Was it only once, was it prolonged? Each horse, each class and each show is a new experience."

In these under-saddle classes begins the gradual transition from the sporthorse in-hand to the dressage horse under saddle. They are yet another stepping-stone along the path toward perfection. ❧

# Chapter Eight
## Hunter In-Hand Classes

The hunter show horse in the United States has a style that is unique to this country. In colonial America, local horseracing grew into what is now Thoroughbred racing. Fox hunting was another early sport that required the same type of agile, graceful horse. As these two sports flourished, Americans took the stock used for these events and developed their own form of hunter. The American Horse Shows Association came into being in 1917 and from that organization, now called USA Equestrian came the many rules now applied to American show hunters competitions.

Hunters differ from sporthorses in both conformation and movement. In a hunter, conformation and movement that is more on the forehand is desirable. Hunters' necks are lower set. Their movement is flat with little or no knee or hock action. They cover a lot of ground with low, sweeping strides, often called "daisy-cutter" movement or "flat-kneed" movement. Instead of moving through the back and having a bouncy, suspended stride, their legs move their bodies quietly. They tend to be easy to ride as the rider glides along with the horse, whereas sitting upper-level dressage movements demand an active role from a rider's entire body.

The way hunters are shown in-hand differs as well. Hunters are presented in a slightly different standing position from sporthorses. The front legs either can be square, with the front hooves parallel and the back hooves parallel, or with the foreleg nearest the judge advanced slightly. The hind leg nearest the judge is the farthest back. The position is usually reversed as the judge walks around the horse. One exception to doing this is when covering up a flaw, such as a toed-out or a sickle hocked horse. If these flaws are covered by the horse's position, the handler should not reposition the horse. The judge will only judge what is seen at the time.

The flat movement typically seen in a hunter is considered by both exhibitors and judges alike to be good movement, and any other type is considered poor movement and will not be rewarded in a hunter class. Most hunters do not track up, nor is it expected of them. What is expected is for a horse's legs to swing back and forth with little bend in the joints. The movement in profile should reach out far and cover a lot of ground, equally in front as well as from behind. From head on and from the rear, the legs of the horse should move straight with no winging, which is when a leg flips out to the side as the horse moves forward, or other distracting deviations. The hooves should strike the ground flat and evenly, not slightly to one side.

A pretty head and neck are important for a hunter's conformation, as is a nicely developed topline. The hunter is longer from nose to tail than a dressage horse. A long, snaky neck in a dressage horse would result in more difficulty collecting, going on the bit and balancing on his haunches. In a hunter, the longer neck is needed to guide him gracefully over fences. To win the class the hunter needs not only the desired movement and conformation, but he also needs to have a well-muscled, mature, developed build. A colt born in June is not likely to win over the one born in January, because the older

*Professional hunter-in-hand handler Mike Rowe and his well-mannered entry enroute to the Futurity. Note the ground-covering "daisy-cutter" movement.*

colt will be larger and more developed. The judge is seeking a horse as near perfection as can be found in the class. Meeting a standard is the goal of these classes. The hunter is not seen as a whole athlete and is not forgiven for flaws that do not hinder his movement. His future potential is disregarded. He is judged only by what he presents that day.

## Hunter In-Hand Patterns

There are two basic patterns used to show hunters in-hand. Futurities, where the breeder of the foal has paid dues periodically since about the time the foal was born, have a slightly different pattern than do the regular breeding classes. All the horses in a futurity enter the ring and stand loosely together at the far end as they await their turn to be judged. One at a time, the horses are walked to the opposite end of the arena to stand for the judge. When asked, the horse is then walked at an angle away from the judge, turned and trotted in profile for the judge, turned again, thus forming a triangle of sorts as he is walked back toward the judge. This is a small, loosely made tri-angle shape and provides easy viewing for the judge.

Once a horse has completed this, the next horse is judged. After each horse has gone through this pattern, the entire class may be asked to trot past the judge, one at a time, for a last look.

In regular hunter in-hand classes, horses enter the arena and line up head to tail to be judged for conformation. The horse in the front is then asked to turn and trot down the long side of the arena toward the judge and then past him or her. The judge turns to watch the horse's departure. The judge may ask for the walk in this way, or may judge the walk as the horses enter the ring. In each pattern the judge may ask for any or all horses to repeat a gait.

In both types of classes, the exhibitor puts forth effort to getting the horse to lower his head and stretch his neck while standing for conformation. The most useful tool for achieving this is a treat such as a handful of grass or small carrots.

There is a third type of hunter in-hand class, but it is only found at registered Appaloosa shows. In this class the horses are shown like dressage horses by walking and trotting on the triangle. In fact, this class was originally intended for Appaloosa breeders who bred dressage-type horses and was offered as an outlet for them to show their product. But the entries soon filled with the modern Appaloosa hunter-type horses, and the judging leaned toward them. As a result, the name of the class was changed but not the pattern of showing. Another difference in these shows is that instead of braiding, the horse's mane is banded, unless he is showing at a world or national show, then he is braided. At the World and National shows, an exhibitor has time to braid because English and Western classes are on different days. At weekend shows the exhibitor is likely to enter both English and Western classes in the same day and does not have time to change from bands to braids.

## Turn Out for Hunter In-Hand Classes

At all A-rated hunter shows, yearlings and older horses are shown in bridles. This rule has fluctuated over the years depending on what is specified in the *USAEq Rule Book*. However, it is generally accepted by exhibitors and judges alike that yearlings must be shown in a bridle or be eliminated from the class. The bridle should be a plain headstall, not too thick or thin, and in a color as close to the horse's color as possible. Most are shown in either D-ring or full cheek snaffles with keepers. Longer reins are beneficial in case the horse rears or otherwise acts up as the handler will be less likely to lose control. Horse reins are used on ponies and yearlings. A leather lead shank with a chain may be used on the bridle in place of reins. Weanlings are shown in a plain leather halter with brass fittings and a chain lead.

Manes and tails should be braided. Braids are always on the right side of the neck, and they usually number between 30–40 to show off the length of the horse's neck. There is one style of braid currently acceptable. It is a tight braid with the top pulled into a slight ball and the bottom flat against the horse's neck (see page 62). The entire mane is braided.

The horse's mane is pulled until it lies flat and evenly on the right side at about $3\frac{1}{2}$ inches long. To braid, wet the mane with a sponge and use a comb to separate a small section of hair to be braided. Secure the rest of the mane out of the way with a hair clip. Separate the hair into three sections and tightly cross each outside section over to the middle to make a braid.

About one-third of the way down incorporate a 12-inch piece of yarn, folded in half, into the two outside sections of hair and continue braiding. The yarn is then used to tie the end of the braid. Yarn is used because it doesn't break the hair like rubber bands can and it makes the finished braid neater. The color of the yarn used should match the color of the horse's mane.

Several types of tools can be used to pull up the yarn to finish the braid. One tool, a braid puller, comes in several different styles. One consists of a smooth oval loop on the end, much like the eye of a needle. The tool is used by sliding it down through the top of the braid where the yarn is fed through the eye. The tool is then pulled back up through the top, bringing the yarn with it. Latch hooks can also be used. They have a hook-like end that opens and closes around the yarn. People have differing opinions as to which is easiest to use, thus one should use whichever is preferred.

Once the yarn is pulled through the top, it is brought under the braid, one strand on each side, crossed and then brought back up again, one strand on each side of the braid. The middle of the braid is pushed toward the horse's crest, making it rise, and then the yarn is tied tightly under that rise. The excess of the yarn is cut.

It takes an experienced braider 25-60 minutes to braid a horse. Even proficient braiders complain of the pain the job causes their hands. Some people use strips of bandage or tape around their fingers to protect them.

One top braider, Ruthann Smith, has overcome the problem of pain and teaches clinics on braiding quickly and neatly without pain. She says, "I teach a formula for braiding. Inherent to the formula is a leverage system between fingers so braids are tight and hands are relaxed. This is how I am able to braid 22 manes or 17 manes and tails per night." She is the designer of a simple but useful apparatus that hangs around her neck, holding her tools and keeping them within easy reach while preventing them from falling to the floor. Ruthann has produced an excellent video, *The Better Braiding Video and Tool System*, available at your local tack shop or at www.luckybraids.com.

A novice braider can take as many as five hours to braid a single horse, and even then the braiding might not be functional. A beginner can take as long as six months to become proficient at braiding. Though many people only braid horses that show in A-rated competitions, all hunter in-hand horses should be braided, regardless of the rating of the show. Braiding is considered a compliment to the judge, and it also enhances the beauty of the horse's neck.

The braids must be neat. Stray, short hairs sticking up along the crest or braids that are not even and in proportion to one another are unattractive. There is no room in competition for the braids of a beginner. People who have never developed the skill should hire someone to braid for them.

Spandex head and neck coverings can help keep hay out of braids overnight and can keep the braids from being rubbed loose, but some horses might be irritated by the cover as much as they are by the tight braids and thus be prone to rubbing more than they might otherwise. Try on the cover days before the show and observe your horse's reaction. Braids should not be left in any longer than they must be because they are tight and can be itchy and irritating.

Hunters' tails are not banged as in dressage classes but left natural and as long as possible. Some tails are never brushed to spare the hairs from breakage. They are washed and then rinsed with a silicone-based conditioner. The tangles are gently separated out by hand. The dock of the tail is always braided for a hunter in-hand class. The forelock of the horse as well as the dock of its tail is French braided. This is similar to regular braids, which use three strands, except that new strands are added as the braid progresses, and the original three strands eventually get left

*A hunter-style braided tail showing neat and precise sections of hair.*

behind as they are woven into the braid by the new strands. This continues until the regular braiding of three strands ends the braid or, in the case of the tail, when the end of the tailbone is reached. On the forelock, the end of the braid is pulled through the main braid with a braid puller and tied neatly. The end of the braid on the tail should be folded in half and the braid sewn in flat, neat and unobtrusive or rolled into a coil.

Hunters are trimmed cleanly on their faces, ears, fetlocks and above their coronet bands, with the occasional exhibitor leaving eye whiskers intact. The bridle path is no wider than the crown piece of the bridle. This makes room for more braids, and therefore makes the length of neck look more elegant.

Hunter's hooves are oiled, never shellacked, as it is thought to look too artificial. White markings on legs are clipped short as they are easier to wash, and cornstarch or talcum powder is rubbed on them to brighten them.

Dress for handlers in hunter in-hand classes is not strict, but judges do have their preferences and they expect participants to look as if they are showing in a horse show. For men, dress pants in colors such as khaki, grey, blue, black or other conservative colors are appreciated as is a blue, green, black or other conservative-color jacket, and a nice shirt and tie.

Women have the option of wearing a conservative-colored shirt with pants or a skirt. They may choose to wear a jacket. A billowing dress with a wide-brimmed hat is not a good choice as either could get in the way of showing and running, especially on windy days.

Riding clothes are not considered proper attire for showing a horse in-hand unless the handler does not have time to change between mounted and in-hand classes. Clothes that are not appreciated are T-shirts, jeans or anything sloppy and overly casual. A riding crop may be carried and used for disciplining unruly horses, but is not used as a showing aid. Gloves are not seen in hunter-in-hand classes. Baseball caps are frequently seen, as are other types of hats.

## A Winning Coat

Grooming, while important for sporthorses, is imperative for the hunter. A fresh from the pasture look will not get any positive notice from the judge. Proper feeding is essential for a sleek horse. A high protein feed of at least 13 percent and a fresh source of forage, either hay, grass or both are the main factors in maintaining a horse's basic health. Supplements can be found in over-the-counter preparations as well as in naturally occuring foods such as raspberry leaves, flaxseed, various oils and so on.

Some horse owners mix mature flaxseeds or flaxseed oil, which are high in essential fatty acids, including the popular Omega-3, in the horse's grain to make his coat shine. Commercial linseed oil, while made from flaxseed is not a pure product and is meant for industrial use, not internal use. Using immature seeds or too much flaxseed can be toxic, though in small amounts flax provides many health benefits. Flaxseed is said to preserve the health of cell walls, enabling them to reach greater longevity and it is thought to help humans avoid degenerative diseases such as arthritis. It is possible that horses reap the same benefits.

Vegetable oils, such as canola, safflower, wheat germ, rice bran, olive oil, etc., can be added to the grain for the purpose of putting a shine on the horse's coat. Oil has the added benefit of preventing grain from becoming compacted inside the horse, which is one of the main causes of colic.

Stinging nettle is an herb that is considered safe to use as a food supplement. When the dried, crumbled nettles are added to grain they provide iron, calcium, potassium, vitamins A and C and are said to bring dapples to the horse's coat. Ongoing research on stinging nettles is finding an endless supply of health benefits this herb can bring.

Red raspberry leaf is an herb that tastes good to horses. It is high in vitamins A, B, C and E, and iron, calcium and phosphorus. It has an excellent reputation for aiding pregnancy and childbirth in both horses and humans.

As of this writing none of these food supplements are prohibited by USA Equestrian or Fédération Equestre Internationale (FEI) rules. However, it is the individual horse owner's responsibility to keep up with any changes in these rules.

In spring and summer, hunter show horses are stall kept by day and turned out at night to keep the sun from fading their coats. Lights are used at night in winter and early spring to make the daylight appear to last longer. This can fool the horse's system into thinking it is spring and induces them to shed. Horses are often blanketed in the evenings from April to June and late August to October, and blanketed all day from November to March to prevent the winter coat from developing to it's fullest. Details, such as the months when blankets are used, the thickness of the blankets, and the length of day they are used vary depending on the climate the horse is in.

# Chapter Nine
## Tips for the Show

### Trailering

A horse should know how to trailer peacefully well in advance of going to his first show. For horses new to trailering or those that have erratic behavior, a head bumper, which is a leather helmet for the horse, can prevent tragedy. Some people use shipping boots, to protect a horse's legs, coronet band and heels, but they are not recommended for foals as they might irritate the animal so that he misbehaves more than he might otherwise. If used, shipping boots should be introduced well in advance to trailering. Any sort of leg wraps must be removed before entering a class.

It is easiest to teach a horse to trailer when he is a foal because most foals will follow their mothers into the trailer and ride quietly with them, especially if they have a few weeks experience in leading prior to being asked to trailer.

If the foal's mother does not trailer well, or if they are separated before the foal learns to trailer, training can be more difficult. It is important to work on space issues and to teach the foal to move forward from both a cluck and with a signal from the whip. Once this training is under way the horse should be willing to go into the trailer when asked, simply because he was asked.

Some horses need a light, steady tap on the rump with a dressage whip to inspire them to enter the trailer. This will only work if the horse has been taught to move away from taps with the whip. When the horse takes a step forward, the tapping must cease. If tapping with the whip continues, even though the horse takes steps forward, the signal is rendered useless.

The best way to create a horse that trailers easily is to start with frequent, short, pleasant trips in the company of horses he gets along with.

## Hooves

Hooves should be trimmed no sooner than two weeks before a show. This gives them time to grow out if they are trimmed too short. If the owner is familiar with the farrier and the farrier has a good track record with trimming that horse's hooves, this precaution may be unnecessary. However, it's probably best to be on the safe side since entry fees are expensive and often nonrefundable.

# Know the Rules

Adherence to rules can make or break a horse and handler's success at a show. When preparing to go to a show or inspection, bring all the rule books and flyers that apply to the show and to any associations linked to it, such as the USAEq. The literature should have been read prior to the show. Any variations in procedures, tack, turnout, dress, etc., should be noted and accounted for.

In addition, the prize list for a particular show will make clear exactly which classes you may be eligible for; these can vary from show to show. There will also be information on any additional rules or situations you should be aware of ahead of time.

When filling out papers and forms, get someone who is experienced to check them over to make sure you have not left something out. There are many forms to fill out especially if signing up for something like USDF All-Breeds Awards or the USDF Breeders Championship Series. Missing just one form or not filling one out properly could cost a year-end placing. Once the forms have been sent to the appropriate associations, call to make sure they have been received and are filled out properly. Do this before going to any shows to avoid losing points. More than once a lost piece of paper or an incomplete form has prevented an exhibiter from getting an award.

# Don't Forget ...

There are obvious things to bring to a show, such as your tack and show clothes. Having extra of these items is useful if something gets soiled or broken. Fly spray, grooming tools, buckets, feed, proof of a current, negative Coggins test, health papers if crossing state lines and blankets are other obvious things to take. Obvious or not, it won't hurt to make a checklist and cross off each item as it is loaded into the tack box, truck or trailer.

There are less obvious items that can make a show more pleasant such as washed fresh fruit or other healthy lunch items, and water to drink. If it is a hot day, a wet, ice-covered towel kept in the cooler will bring instant relief to an overheated person. Also bring extra shoes and socks in case a pair becomes wet.

Bringing a jug of water for wetting a sponge to either fix a braid or wipe off dirt, or even for offering the horse a drink can be more convenient and time saving than searching for a water source at the show ground. The horse also may appreciate having familiar-tasting water. Some horses won't drink strange water and could risk dehydration.

An old sock and a jar of olive or some other oil can be used to brighten boots, bridles and horse's manes, tails, and faces. Even a light amount applied to his shoulders, legs and hindquarters brings out extra shine and highlights. Use this sparingly to avoid making streaks or creating a magnet for dust. A little goes a long way.

Something that should be under or behind the truck seat at all times is a first aid kit or two. One for people can be purchased already filled with items. One for horses can also be purchased and should include several Vetrap/3M-type bandages, a twitch (in case an emergency requires immediate restraint of the horse), electrolytes, a flashlight, antibacterial ointment such as Neosporin, an antiseptic, a liniment such as witch hazel (good for treatment of bruises and sprains), gauze, butazolidin (avoid using bute until after a veterinarian's exam, but it can be useful to have on hand) and a thermometer.

## Show Checklist

**For the Horse:**

Blankets
Bridle or halter and leather lead with a chain for showing
Brushes and braiding materials
Buckets
Coggins test
Drinking water
Extra halter, in case of breakage
First aid kit
Fly spray
Feed
Head bumper
Health papers
Hoof dressing
Leg wraps
Old sock and oil
Shipping boots
Silicone mane/tail/coat spray

Sponge
Tail bag/wrap

**For the Handler:**

Cell phone
Cooler, ice and towel
Dressage whip
Drinking water with cups
Emergency numbers
Extra shoes
First aid kit
Fruit or other snack items
Lunge wWhip
Money
Pants
Polo shirt (or two)
Rule books
Show flyer
Socks, two pair
Hat/sunscreen
Bug repellant

# Chapter Ten
## Trouble Shooting

No matter what training method a handler uses there will be, at some point, a horse that is difficult or uncooperative in one way or another, and there will be a tendency for a novice to make classic mistakes. Here are some helpful hints to avoid pitfalls, both large and small.

## Bullies

Some young colts will not leave people alone who come into their pastures for whatever reason. They nip, rear and swing around their rear ends to kick and generally harass anyone they see. As in their herd structure, these colts are trying out for dominant status. However, they must be discouraged from acting this way around humans, because it is dangerous for the handlers.

Using the butt end of a dressage whip to define your space will help considerably. If the young horse approaches, swing the butt end of the whip at the outermost boundary of your space like a pendulum, face-level to the young horse. Instead of swinging it outward to point toward your destination, swing it sideways to indicate an imaginary fence between you and the colt. Appear to not pay attention to the animal, though be aware of any threatening advances he may be planning.

If, out of curiosity or devilment, he proceeds to invade your space, he will be struck. Be wary of retaliation in the form of spinning haunches. If they are offered, punish him smartly and stay out of his aim. After a few days, he should learn to be respectful in his approach.

Do not wait for a horse to bite or kick and then go after him with the whip. The whip is to be used as a "do not enter" sign. If the colt refuses to obey the sign, he punishes himself.

## Fixing Goof-ups on the Triangle

Two main hindrances are caused by the inexperienced handler. One is dragging the horse's head around to one side while walking or trotting due to clutching the reins too close. The other is not running fast enough. For the latter, the cure is for the handler to speed up. Some people are inclined to jog, but that is not a fast enough gait for showing a horse on the triangle. If the handler does not feel physically able to run fast enough to keep up with her horse, perhaps hiring a professional for the important shows and inspections is the best option for presenting the horse at its best.

The reins or lead rope should be loose during both the walk and the trot. If they are taut the horse's carriage, rhythm and straightness can be thrown off. Practice with a well-trained horse that can be trusted. Lead him on a loose rein and be aware of any tendency to clench the reins. Even while

*The reins here are so long that if the horse became uncooperative, there would be little the handler could do to prevent it. Long reins are common in hunter-in-hand classes, and the horses are usually cooperative enough to allow it.*

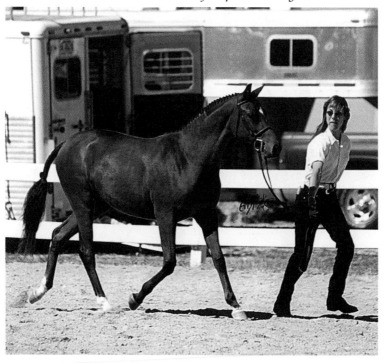

standing the handler should practice having the horse stand on a loose rein. The horse must have the freedom of his head and neck to present himself well. If space issues have been sorted out and the horse has learned to respect his handler as the herd boss, running beside him on a loose rein should come easily.

A handler also should be aware of having the reins too loose. If she brings the reins back to the horse's shoulder and they are still slack, then they are too loose to give any control.

Experienced handlers can maintain rein contact with-

*If the reins are held too far from the horse's mouth, control will be lost if the horse misbehaves. Head carriage can affect the horse's movement, as can be seen when this horse's head is pulled to one side.*

out pulling the horse's head off course. They use this contact to give the horse half halts and to turn the horse at the corners. If a handler wishes to hold the reins this way she will need to practice. Her hands need to be steady and to apply the same light contact that a rider under saddle is expected to apply. Just like the person learning to post who yanks the reins and horse's mouth upward with every stride, only practice will give someone a steady enough hand to maintain gentle, effective contact.

One goof up that does not have to be a big deal is when the horse breaks into a canter rather than showing off

*A good example of contact without interference from the reins.*

a fabulous trot. It can become a big deal if the handler punishes the horse. A horse punished or brought down to a walk abruptly will be less enthusiastic when asked to trot. He will hold back, afraid of doing something wrong. The handler needs only to bring the horse down from the canter gently by raising up her left hand to signal the horse to slow down while she continues moving forward and stays at the horse's shoulder and proceeds with the trot.

Regardless of whether the horse is being shown to promote his sire or to expose him to life in the show ring, the owner should not become discouraged if the horse does not place first. Breeders whose product does not win might be tempted to discontinue their breeding program, but there are two things to keep in mind before making that decision:

Horses that win in large in-hand classes are likely to be those with an extravagant trot. That same trot has little to do with what is needed to make a finished Grand Prix horse. Disposition, training and excellent riding are the main three factors in that equation.

Another thing to keep in mind is that even if a breeder is not turning out Grand Prix horses, there is still a market to tap. The market for a Grand Prix horse is very small. The vast majority of dressage riders are riding at the lower levels.

Showing a horse for the reason of exposing him to shows is an excellent reason to take the horse in-hand. For the owner who does not need to promote a horse but has a young animal to show, the results of the horse's placing will not matter as much since the owner will keep in mind the important factors that rest in their own hands that can determine the future.

As beneficial as showing in-hand can be for a young horse, if competing to win becomes the main focus of showing it is probably best to refrain from showing a very young horse in-hand. Temptation to overwork the foal, possibly stall him for benefit of his coat and lunge him at too young an age

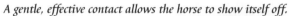

*A gentle, effective contact allows the horse to show itself off.*

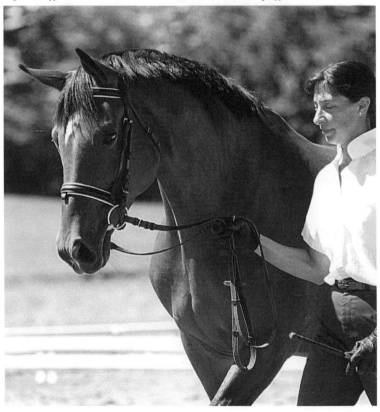

will do nothing to enhance the horse's future, and may well damage him.

There is great satisfaction in being in the company of a beautiful, proud being that moves with you as a partner. The beauty of this relationship can begin well before a saddle crosses the horse's back.

I wish you every success.

# Photo Credits